ALIEN GODS
ON AMERICAN TURF

ALIEN GODS
ON
AMERICAN TURF

TERRY MUCK

VICTOR BOOKS®
A DIVISION OF SCRIPTURE PRESS PUBLICATIONS INC.
USA CANADA ENGLAND

All Scripture quotations are from the Holy Bible, New International Version, © 1973, 1978, 1984, International Bible Society. Used by permission of Zondervan Bible Publishers.

Cover illustration: Tim Jonke

Library of Congress Cataloging-in-Publication Data

Muck, Terry C., 1947–
Alien gods on American turf / by Terry Muck.
   p. cm.—(Christianity Today series)
   Includes bibliographical references.
   ISBN 0-89693-545-0
   1. United States—Religion—1960– 2. Religious pluralism—United States—History—20th century.
   3. Evangelistic work—United States. 4. Witness
   bearing (Christianity) I. Title. II. Series.
BL2525.M83   1990
200'.973—dc20   89-78264
                                             CIP

1 2 3 4 5 6 7 8 9 10 Printing/Year 94 93 92 91 90

CONTENTS

To my sons,
David, Paul, and Joseph,
who are growing up
in the religious world
this book describes.

PROLOGUE

When people ask 6′2″ blue-eyed Jim Minter where he goes to church, he usually stops them short, stating, "I'm a Hindu."

There aren't a lot of Hindus in Chillicothe, Ohio, where Minter and his wife, Sadhna, live. If you ask a local gas-station attendant for directions to the nearest Hindu temple, chances are very good you will get a blank stare in return.

"When I tell people at work I'm a Hindu, I get a variety of reactions: surprise, then a pause to see if I'm joking, then curiosity. They don't know many chemists who are practicing Hindus, I guess."

Minter is a Hindu by choice. There is no other way he could have become one. He grew up in a Southern Baptist minister's home, studied and read a great deal about Christianity in college, still deeply appreciates the teachings of Jesus and the lessons of the Old Testament, and maintains deep friendships with committed Christians. But as for him and his house, they are Hindus.

The story of his choice is in many ways the story of this book.

Minter grew up in the home of his grandfather, a minister whom Minter describes as "hardshell Southern Baptist." "I thought everyone in the world was Southern Baptist and toed the line just as I did," he remembers.

Minter's life changed when he went to college, first at Old Dominion University in Norfolk, Virginia, and then at Virginia Commonwealth in Richmond. Both were city schools with large numbers of international students. The cosmopolitan atmosphere made Minter see a new world beyond his traditional Southern Baptist boundaries.

Minter remembers particularly his discussions with the local Hare Krishna commune. "I was attracted by the tenets of what they believed. Their goal was peace and relaxation, achieved by following a teacher instructing them in the chanting of a phrase that helped focus their thoughts on spiritual things. I liked their morality: faithfulness in sexual relationships, and no meat, alcohol, or drugs of any kind.

"But I quickly saw they weren't perfect by any means. Many of them were just as mindless and blindly obedient to men as some Christians I knew. I concluded that separation from society—by either Christians or Hindus—didn't work. It only avoided the problems of living spiritually in an imperfect age."

After graduation Minter took up his career as a research chemist. He recognizes in retrospect that he definitely put his career ahead of his spiritual search. Still, he applied some of his observations of American corporate life to the Christianity that he couldn't quite make work for himself.

"I decided that there were two aspects to all religion: the organizational and the personal. In the West we have dichotomized the two and overemphasized the organizational. This has contributed to an intellectual laziness about the spiritual life that scares me."

Minter's life truly changed when he met Sadhna.

"I went to a barber and cosmetology school to get a haircut. It was one of those places where students practice on the public. The student assigned to cut my hair was this beautiful, chocolate-skinned woman. I asked her for her phone number. But when I called, a man (her brother) answered and said she didn't live there.

"About eight weeks later I needed another haircut. Again I was assigned to this beautiful woman. This time I learned her name—Sadhna. I asked for her number again, and this time when I called, she answered. I invited her to a play. But she couldn't go. So again I backed off.

"Two months later my hair needed attention again—and for the third time she was assigned to cut my hair. You must realize that thirty-six students were randomly assigned to cut people's hair. The chances of me getting this woman three times in a row were something like one in three or four million. I decided a higher power had a hand in this.

"This time when I asked her for a date, she accepted. Over the course of several months we fell in love and were married."

Sadhna was an immigrant from India, a Hindu of high Brahman caste. Her first husband had been killed in India in a car crash, and she had come to the United States because life for a widow is difficult in India. Still, her family ties were close, and she asked Minter to go to India for a traditional Hindu wedding.

"It was that experience, along with a great deal of reading and thinking, that made me decide to become a Hindu. I liked what I saw of Hinduism in India: a close family, a wedding service with specific, practical vows; an integration of personal and public faith—many things impressed me. And I read widely in sacred Hindu texts: the Bhagavad-Gita, the Ramayana, the writings of Swami Vivekananda. All of them confirmed my thinking. This seemed to be a religion that actually allowed one to live out the best in the teachings of Jesus. Christianity didn't."

So how does Minter live now? He occasionally goes to a Hindu temple when he feels the need. He has a strong desire to continue to grow in faith. This may lead, he thinks, to a one- or two-year sabbatical from his career to go to India to study with a teacher. "I really feel in charge of my life now. I'm responsible before God to grow in faith. I want to take that responsibility seriously.

"I read the Old and New Testaments. I still have good relationships with some of my old Christian friends. I miss interaction with more Hindus. There aren't enough here. But I do have Sadhna.

"Frankly, I don't find many really religious people at all. Most are beyond even agnosticism. Most are terminally apathetic. Having that happen is my biggest fear. But I'm very happy with the direction my faith is taking me. I believe we will all eventually be judged by the fruits of our lives. I think my Hindu beliefs will make me the most spiritually fruitful person I can be."

Why do people like Jim Minter choose to convert to a world religion like Hinduism? What are the factors that make this decision possible? Are there others like him? Do many American Christians follow his path, or is he a rarity?

If Jim Minter stories are becoming more common, what, if anything, should we do about it? How should we relate to the followers of other world religions—especially when their numbers are increasing?

I hope to answer these questions in this book. The influences that affected Jim Minter are increasingly affecting others. A serious challenge lies ahead. And there are steps we can take to meet it head-on.

Terry Muck

Chapter 1

THE INVISIBLE
CRISIS

Times change. In the first census taken in our country in 1790, almost none of the nearly four million people counted were Asian. Almost all were of Western European ancestry. By the tenth United States census in 1880, only 100,000 Asians were among the fifty million people counted. By the time of the 1970 census, however, the number of Asians had jumped to over one million, with another 720,000 in a nonwhite category that included Filipinos, Indians, and other immigrants. In ninety years, our population had increased fourfold, yet the number of Asians alone had increased tenfold.[1]

Immigrants usually bring their religion with them, so this growth in non-European immigrants has had a significant effect on our country's religious mix.[2] Asian immigrants have brought Hinduism and several varieties of Buddhism to American shores. Middle Eastern immigrants have brought Islam. Immigrants have introduced numerous other religions from Africa, South America, and Oceania. The religious make-up of the United States has become as varied as the skin colors of our new immigrants.

Everything points to this trend continuing. Ask people at work or in your neighborhood. Almost everyone knows someone who belongs to a non-Christian faith. Check the phone book of any medium to large American city. There is almost sure to be a Muslim mosque listed. Nearly as likely there is also a Buddhist or Hindu temple. *The Encyclopedia of American Religions* lists more than 1,500 distinct religious groups in America: 900 have Christian roots; 600, non-Christian roots.[3] Demographic and religious experts predict the trend will increase; no one suggests that America will return to being the Christian monolith it was in 1790. An already bewildering variety of religions, cults, and world views is sure to grow even more confusing.

Yet here is a strange reality: for most American Christians this trend just does not create an impression. Scholars and demographers talk about it incessantly. But for the average man on the street, it is at most a curious fact. In a recent survey, *Christianity Today* magazine asked a cross section of its readership to name the ten toughest questions facing American Christianity. The challenge of the world religions did not even register.[4] Similarly, a recent Gallup poll asked American citizens to name their areas of greatest concern for the coming years. Few mentioned the growing religious diversity in our country.[5]

An urban phenomenon

Why doesn't this trend register? One reason is that the influx of the world religions has centered in cities. "Migration over the past century and a half has been largely a city-ward movement," writes demographer David Ward.[6] Immigrant communities find it easier to settle and establish new roots in cities.

Our cities are in trouble. Poverty, homelessness, crime, drugs, impotent educational systems, ethnic conflicts—the list goes on and on.[7] Out of necessity, urbanites have developed expertise at skirting all but the most essential issues. The influx of world religions ranks far down the list in terms of demanding attention. In urban sensory overload, Muslims, Buddhists, and Hindus are like furniture we grow accustomed to in our houses. The grandfather clock ticks faithfully in the corner and chimes on the hour, but we don't hear it.

If world religions go unnoticed by city dwellers, they are practically invisible to Americans in suburban or rural areas. For them, the realities of city life are to be avoided or escaped. They may drive through the city, but they seek no intimate contact with it. Mosques and temples are not out of sight, but they are out of mind. That is where the world religions have stayed—out of consciousness. As long as the followers of an Indian guru do their proselytizing on a downtown street corner or in the corridors of a major airport, they remain part of the scenery. But as soon as they go rural, we notice.

In 1981 a 50-year-old Hindu guru, Bhagwan Shree Rajneesh, bought 64,229 acres of land in Antelope, Oregon, and established a commune. At first he won grudging acceptance from the community. But when he tried to take over the local political process so he could grant his commune special building and zoning permits, people rejected the *ashram*. And when stories of free love and unconditional obedience about the commune became publicly known, opposition stiffened. Eventually Swami Rajneesh was forced to leave the United States under suspicion of several major crimes. The fallout for mainline Hindus around the country was significant. Temples that for years had peacefully coexisted in urban settings had to calm fears by denying that they practiced aberrant forms of Hinduism like the Swami Rajneesh.[8]

A more common situation brings world religions to public attention when they run up against the most sacred of all American cows, the suburban building code. This scenario was played out in Aurora, Illinois, in 1983. A group of Indian professionals, doctors, and engineers met and decided to build a Hindu temple for their worship. The people of Aurora—mostly typical middle Americans—objected, citing possible violations of city building regulations. Eventually the Indians won their right to build, but only after a protracted, sometimes heated battle in city council hearings.[9]

Such stories are so rare as to sound exotic. But they will probably not stay so rare. World religions have centered in the cities, but what is urban today may become suburban tomorrow. Think, for example, how Chinese restaurants, once found only in urban Chinatowns, have become a standard feature of suburbia. The spread of world religions will not stay forever in the city.

Lack of influence

A second reason for the world religions' invisibility is their basic lack of influence. They know they are a minority, strangers in a foreign land, even if they are white Anglos converted to a non-Christian faith. As such, most take a decidedly low-key approach. In general, immigrants are good, quiet citizens.

Politically, adherents of the world religions have little clout in the United States. Few hold elected office. Of the 100 United States senators and 435 members of the House of Representatives, exactly zero percent claim to belong to one of the world's major faiths other than Christianity or Judaism.[10] Although their numbers are growing, members of religious communities do not vote in a bloc, if they vote at all. Most are more concerned about simple economic survival than political power.

Thus, economic power will probably develop before political power does. But even that seems far in the future. The exceptions, of course, are the Japanese and Chinese communities, particularly on the West Coast. Even their economic success, however, has not yet translated into cultural influence. For example, a recent study showed that disproportionately few Asians are represented on television programming, particularly as news anchors and broadcasters.[11]

Neither Chinese nor Japanese Americans represent a particularly coherent religious force, either. In both cultures, religion is a mixed bag, representing Buddhism of several varieties, Confucianism, animism, Shinto, and Taoism. A single individual often embraces a variety of these religious forms. As economic power grows, the likelihood that it will be used to propagate a specific religion is not immediate. America's civil religion remains Christianity.[12]

This absence of political and economic power is not to say that the world religions have no influence. Awareness that Hindus, Buddhists, and Muslims are present and growing is starting to make an impact on American consciousness. Sunday-morning newspapers feature an increasing number of such churches in urban and suburban communities. More and more public high schools teach classes on world religions, and part of the curriculum details the worldwide, Westward spread of these traditions. Such descriptions, however, still evoke curiosity rather than thoughtful consideration.

Thoughtful consideration will only come when the world religions begin making converts. And that has not happened in significant numbers—yet. Exceptions may be noted. In the 1960s numbers of inner-city blacks converted to Islam. Membership in such "Black Muslim" churches may have reached as many as two million, half of the Muslim population in the United States. Today some Japanese Buddhist sects, such as the Nichiren Shoshu, are making similar inroads into urban populations. But on balance, world religions still derive the bulk of their numbers from immigrant populations.

In one key area, the world religions are making significant inroads: the arena of ideas. Eastern, monistic, relativistic ways of thinking are becoming more and more common in our everyday ways of thinking. These ideas are like the wooden forms into which the concrete of religious institutions and beliefs will later be poured. As wooden forms they appear temporary and odd—New Age, cults, obscure philosophical exercises carried out by esoterics with strange names like Baba Free John and Ram Das. But once the forms are firm and the concrete takes the shape of traditional religious institutions, our minds will be more inclined to accept whatever ideas they bring. They will become fixtures on the American scene, uncritically accepted, perhaps even embraced.

The prospects for this depend to a large extent on the religions' ability to adjust their beliefs to a strange setting. Consider, for example, the Islamic community's attempts to adjust to a Western culture that thwarts Islam's five-times-daily prayers, strict separation of the sexes in education, recreation, and worship, and many other moral regulations. Before changes in influence can take place, an American form of Islam must emerge. That will take time.[13] But we ought not to think that the world religions will stay on the political, economic, and cultural margins forever. As their numbers grow, their economic success will increase. With economic success will come cultural adaptation and expanded influence. Part of that influence is certain to be religious.

Our enlightened ethos

A third reason why the growth of world religions causes little
concern is that Americans are a people committed to tolerance, to a
philosophy of "live and let live." As children of the eighteenth-
century Enlightenment, we embrace wholeheartedly the concept of
intellectual tolerance—you believe what you want to believe, I'll
believe what I want to believe, and it makes no difference if our
beliefs are intellectually incompatible. Such tolerance is seen not
only as our intellectual heritage, but also as our religious heritage. It
is seen by many as a logical outgrowth of the Christian doctrine of
love for one's fellow man. If you love people, don't you have to love
and respect their religion?

Unfortunately, in applying the concept of tolerance so broadly we
end up with fuzzy, often conflicting definitions of the word. Before
we can develop an effective policy toward the world religions, we
must define this nettlesome word. When we say *tolerance*, do we
mean an attitude toward people? Do we mean a mutual acceptance
of ideas? Where do we place the concept of tolerance on our
hierarchy of values? Is it more important than commitment to
truth? Than personal development? As Anson Phelps Stokes noted in
his monumental study of church/state relationships, "Religious
tolerance does not necessarily prevent the positive assertion of belief
in one's own church or creed. Intolerance develops only when the
assertion represents a dogmatic conviction which holds one goal or
method or belief with exclusive emphasis and is unwilling to recognize that others have equal rights to their different convictions."[14]

Our all-embracing, benign tolerance of the world religions probably stems from an unconscious sense of superiority. For generations
the world religions have been merely a curiosity. An occasional
eccentric might embrace them, but most Americans never dreamed
that men and women of alien dress and customs would challenge
their view of life. Now, however, events have outdated this attitude.
We will be forced to take the world religions seriously, and that will
force us to sharpen our understanding of tolerance.

Programmed view of the cults

Finally, a reason that is almost paradoxical to the preceding one: We
have transferred our attitude toward cults to the major religious

traditions. The temptation is to relegate Hinduism, Buddhism, and Islam to the same dustbin into which we have cast crystals, pyramids, astrology, talismans, phrenology, Ouija boards, and the 1,001 other odd ducks of religious esotericism.

This temptation is a mistake. Cults tend to die quickly because of their narrowness. If they don't die quickly, that same narrowness limits their growth because of its exclusivistic, inward-looking mentality. By their very nature, cults are not a threat to the long-term health of the major religions, even if they are a major threat to individual young people. Like unsightly pimples, cults can be cosmetically covered and contained until they go away of their own natural causes.

That is not so with the major religions. Hinduism, Buddhism, and Islam claim 700, 300, and 900 million worldwide adherents respectively.[15] They are centuries old, and they will not go away. They offer intellectual respectability and cultural durability. They are all missionary-minded religions, whether they admit it or not. In one form or another, they will be with us in the United States in increasing numbers for years to come. And they will be too large to cover with make-up. They are now a permanent feature of the face of American religion.

Should we be concerned?
Ten or twenty years from now, the full force of non-Christian religions will be felt. They will be established features of our religious terrain, gaining both political and economic influence. Their underlying philosophical ideas will probably, by then, seem as American as shish kebab.

Signs of change are already occurring. In 1987 the first Buddhist chaplain was named to the American armed forces. Buddhists, sensing the need for a central institution to represent the bewildering variety of Buddhist sects in America, formed the American Buddhist Congress. Muslims already have such an organization, the Federation of Islamic Associations. And Hindus are moving in that direction.

Currently we have no philosophy or theology that adequately deals with the presence of the world religions in our midst. Few American Christians know how to respond to a Buddhist or Hindu or

Muslim challenge, except to smile and nod. Our missions strategy assumes that world religions are found overseas, not at home. Our theology of religious tolerance and our legal practice of religious pluralism assume Christianity as the dominant religion, "tolerating" the presence of others—an assumption that our country's courts have failed to endorse. It seems unlikely that this legal trend will be reversed, no matter how many conservative Supreme Court justices are seated, and how many conservative Christian legislators are elected. Given the increased number of Asian immigrants in our country, we must expect to see a heightened visibility for the non-Christian world religions. We must face up to the fact of a religiously plural culture.

Chapter 2

NEW
NEIGHBORS

At first Molly Neff didn't think too much about the foreign boys in her ethnically diverse high school class. But Balu Natarajan was different from any of the other Caucasians, blacks, or Asians. Molly learned that Balu and his family were practicing Hindus.

"I really got to know Balu through the debate team," remembers Molly. "Before one meet I noticed he was very nervous. So I went over and encouraged him. That was the beginning of a good friendship."

The first thing she discovered about Balu's Hindu religion was the effect it had on his behavior. He wouldn't touch alcohol. His moral values were conservative. Molly found this attractive.

"It's funny, but some of the things Balu did were things Christians pay lip service to but don't do. Here was a person from a foreign religion actually doing better at what we said we'd like to do but for one reason or another don't."

Not everything was so attractive, however. There were some unfamiliar statues and images in Balu's house—and where many high school students hang memorabilia from their car's rearview mirror, Balu hung an image of his Hindu deity.

"It's hard to put your finger on it exactly, but he did view life just a little bit differently from my other friends. He was much more accepting of the supernatural roots of everything that happened. We *talked* about God's will being done, but Balu really believed that everything that happened had a supernatural cause."

Molly found her friendship with Balu to be a very positive experience: "When we would get into conversations about subjects that were pretty deep (like God and the purpose of life), it really forced me to think about what I believed. It was different from talking about those things with my Christian friends. When I would talk to them, it was like we all believed the same things and it depended on how we felt that day whether or not we agreed with everything we'd been taught or not.

"With Balu it was different. I remember one time I had a problem with things that were going on on the debate team, and I was talking to Balu about them one night on the phone. He agreed that our team had problems. At one point I said, 'I just don't know what to do.'

" 'You're a Christian, right?' he said.

"I said, 'Yes.'

" 'Christians pray, don't they?' Again I admitted it.

" 'Okay, then; so pray.'

"It makes you a little ashamed that someone of a different religion has to remind you of your own teachings. But in other ways, it's good. That forced me to really define what I believed—and kept me accountable to act on it."

The overall result for Molly was a broadening one. "I saw that there was a whole range of possibilities about the way you could think about the most basic questions of life. That helped me to see that not everyone agreed on the answers to some of these questions, and that being a Christian meant you had to make hard choices. It helped me find my place in terms of who I am in this world and put a whole new value on some of the things I believed."

Did it create any problems for Molly? "I must admit the relationship did raise some questions. It forced me to think about what is essential to my faith and what is not essential. I never really thought about that in detail before. It also forced me to ask the question about how I can relate to people who don't believe the way I do. I had to question what my Christian responsibility to these people is. Am I supposed to give them a hard-sell evangelism every time I meet them? Or, am I really just supposed to be a friend and hope that they see that the way I behave as a Christian makes me different? Is that enough to make them want to know more about my faith?"

How many are there?

If the statistics we read are even reasonably accurate, increasing numbers of American young people (and adults) are going through experiences like Molly's with Balu. More and more people who believe in world religions other than Christianity are moving to, and living in, the United States.

For several reasons, exact figures are hard to come by. First, religions such as Hinduism, Buddhism, and Islam are still relatively unorganized in this country. Immigrants who come with these faiths typically have a strong desire to fit in and adapt to their new culture. Although they do not abandon their religious traditions, some downplay their faith as they seek to succeed in their professions and adjust to a new culture. Second, many of their religious practices are performed in the privacy of homes. Temples and mosques are being built, but that tends not to be a priority. Third, the definition of Hindu, Buddhist, or Muslim is not always strictly religious. It may also be defined culturally or ethnically. Finally, statistics about how many Hindus, Buddhists, and Muslims are in the United States can be exaggerated or just plain inaccurate. Many times the figures include cultic groups (like the Black Muslims) that really don't represent pure Hindu, Buddhist, and Islamic traditions.[1]

There is enough consistency in the statistics, however, to safely say that growth in these groups is accelerating. Perhaps the fastest growing of the three are the Muslims. Immigration has been the primary cause of this growth. Recent figures show not only increased numbers of immigrants, but a definite change in their characteristics.

Islamic Immigration

In *Islamic Values in the United States*, Yvonne Haddad tells us that Muslims have come to the United States in several migratory waves.[2] The first began in 1875 and ended just before World War I. These immigrants were largely uneducated and unskilled young Arabs from rural Syria, Jordan, Palestine, and Lebanon. They came to the United States to escape poor economic conditions in their home countries, and they tended to find jobs as factory workers, miners, and independent merchants. The second wave began in 1918 after World War I and lasted until 1922. Mostly relatives of the earlier immigrants, they were joining their kin who had had a chance to establish an economic base in the United States. The third wave began after World War II, lasting from 1947 to 1960. They came not only from the Middle East, but also from India, Pakistan, Eastern Europe, and the Soviet Union. This wave of immigrants tended to be drawn more from the urban elite. Highly educated, they immediately established a middle-class representation here.

A final surge of immigration, one we are still experiencing, began in 1967 with the relaxation of some immigration laws. For economic and political reasons, this attracted Muslims from all of the above-mentioned countries, many from the educated, professional classes— doctors, lawyers, and engineers.

A concurrent phenomenon with this influx of Muslims from around the world was the growth of Black Muslims in the United States. In the 1960s, urban blacks rejected white America's Christian theology. They became Black Muslims not so much to embrace traditional Islam as to reject a form of Christianity that they saw as racist. One of the early leaders of this movement, Malcolm X, preached a gospel of black superiority. He founded the Nation of Islam and used the religious ideology of the Qur'an to preach a gospel of separation and power to blacks eager to hear such a message. Unfortunately, the message created as much separation and fragmentation *within* the black community as without, and Malcolm X was assassinated in 1965. He was replaced by Elijah Muhammad, who attempted to move the Black Muslims toward orthodox Islam. He took a pilgrimage to Mecca and espoused orthodox Sunni theology.[3] The movement is still in the throes of trying to "go legitimate." It claims a million and a half adherents, probably half of the total U.S. Islamic population.

That population is variously estimated at 1.8 to 4.6 million people, a "denomination" larger than either the Assemblies of God or the Episcopal Church in the United States.[4] Worldwide, Islam has 900 million adherents, a little over 17 percent of the world's population. That is still only half as many as the world's Christian population, but Islam is easily the world's fastest-growing religion. The U.S. figures reflect that vitality. There are currently several studies under way to measure more accurately the number of Muslims in the United States. Figures quoted tend to suffer from the "evangelistically speaking" syndrome. The figures can vary widely according to the ideological stance of the census taker. For example, on the one hand, David Barrett, a conservative Christian statistician and author of *The World Christian Encyclopedia*, estimates there are only 1.8 million Muslims in America. On the other hand, the Islamic Society of North America estimates there are 4.6 million.[5]

Growing numbers of Hindus

The number of Hindus in the United States is not quite so startling. Like Islam, Hinduism has only about a hundred-year history in the United States. But unlike Islam, early Hindu immigrants were strongly discriminated against. Growth has only increased in recent years with the relaxed immigration laws.[6]

An early period of immigration occurred in 1912, when a middle-class group from India settled in San Francisco. They were not particularly well received, and as their numbers grew, some American citizens became alarmed. *Collier's National Weekly* published an article entitled "Hindu Invasion," an alarmist piece wondering what the end would be to this "invasion."[7] A Hindu traveler of the day reflected his feelings about the anxieties raised by such articles: "Well, they are amazingly nervy, these country people. They are so inquisitive. True it is not very annoying when you get used to their ways; but yet, at the same time you cannot help noticing that it is just in their bones to make other people's affairs their own at the shortest possible notice. They are frankly and openly interested in the brightness of your teeth, the color of your hair, the price of your wearing apparel. They will think nothing of pulling out your watch chain, weighing it, measuring it, and confidently asking *What did you give for that?"*

Fears of Indian immigration led Congress to pass the Immigration Acts of 1917 and 1921, and finally the Johnson-Reed Act of 1924 that disallowed Indians from moving to the United States and becoming citizens. Indians already here but not yet naturalized citizens were deported, and severe restrictions were put on the few who remained. Marriage laws discriminated against Indians, and cinema stereotypes made them appear racially inferior. It was only in 1946 that the Luce-Cellar Bill passed Congress, giving Indians the right to U.S. citizenship. Finally, in 1965, the New Immigration Act eliminated the quota system altogether. It was only then that the Hindu temple tradition in the United States really began to grow.

Hinduism's presence nonetheless imprinted the American consciousness through several sources. During the difficult years of discrimination, the major sources were from charismatic personalities such as Ramakrishna and his major disciple, Vivekananda (founder of the Vedanta Society). They taught a Westernized version of Hindu philosophy that preached the oneness of all religions. It was Vivekananda who gave a stirring address at the 1893 Parliament of World Religions at the Chicago World's Fair, capturing the imagination of many religious seekers here in the United States.

Mahatma Gandhi further raised the American consciousness to Hinduism while being involved in political and cultural attempts to free India from British rule. More recently, various swamis and gurus from India have come to the United States with popularized versions of Hinduism. Swami Prabhupada brought to our shores the International Society for Krishna Consciousness, which is more commonly known as the Hare Krishna movement. He was followed by Maharishi Mahesh Yogi, who brought a version of meditation and yoga called Transcendental Meditation (TM), appealing widely to many countercultural groups in the 1960s.

Despite the multitude of Americans who have converted to Hinduism, the number of Hindus in the United States is still sharply tied to Indian immigrant populations. Approximately 100,000 Indians, for example, are in metro New York. Since Hinduism is as much an ethnic/nationalistic identification as a religion, we can confidently count them as Hindu although the level of religious commitment among them probably varies widely. Some inroads have also been made among Western populations, especially through more intellectual Hindu approaches as the Vedanta Society, which teaches a form of Hinduism that appeals to philosophers and global religionists.

Buddhists from East and West
Buddhists have come to the United States from both the East and the West. Western contact with Buddhism originally came from European explorers, such as the Portuguese in Ceylon, the Portuguese and Spanish in China, and the British in China. At first this fairly superficial contact was limited to trade. It did lead, however, to follow-up missionary contact, which led to an initial understanding of Buddhism. European universities began to study Oriental religions, a movement that eventually reached American shores in the form of scholarly and academic interaction.

An idealized form of Buddhism found a home among the transcendentalists of New England. Ralph Waldo Emerson had read both the Upanishads and the Bhagavad-Gita, early Hindu scriptures. With this knowledge as a base, he read great Buddhist writings and found them intellectually exciting. The Theosophical Society, begun in 1897 by Madam Blavatsky, also gained a foothold on the East Coast and helped further promote the ideas of Buddhism. Western European scholars began to study the Buddhist languages Pali and Sanskrit, and that interest opened the doors to a few Westerners actually adopting the religious faith of Buddhism, particularly Theravada Buddhism, centering largely on Buddhist meditation techniques.

Probably the more significant influx of Buddhism, at least in terms of numbers, came from the East. An immigrant Buddhist faith began largely when the United States started trading with Japan and China. The 1860 California Gold Rush brought hundreds of thousands of Chinese laborers to California. Those numbers, however, did not immediately mean hundreds of thousands of Buddhists. The Chinese version of Buddhism is an amalgamation of Buddhism, Confucianism, and Taoism. Chinese immigrant religion tended to be remarkably diverse and undefined. If only a small percentage of these Chinese immigrants could be viewed as Buddhists, however, that still is a significant number.

A more important influx of Buddhists came from Japanese immigrants. After the postwar occupation of Japan, many Japanese found a home in the United States and brought with them an almost bewildering variety of schools of Buddhism, including Zen, Nichiren Shoshu, and Jodo Shinshu. And from Tibet came Tantric Buddhism or Vajrayana Buddhism.

Today, Buddhism as an organized religion is coming of age in the United States. In 1988 the World Fellowship of Buddhists, the international umbrella group representing all the world's schools of Buddhism, met for the first time in the United States in Los Angeles. Significantly, Buddhist leaders recognized that Buddhism had evolved as a major religion in the United States.

Estimates varied at that conference about the number of U.S. Buddhists, but with over one thousand Buddhist organizations, a figure as high as four million seems reasonable. Although still a very small percentage of the world's 250 million Buddhists, it is a rapidly growing number.[8]

Two challenges

Demographics indicate that the growth of Hinduism, Buddhism, and Islam will continue. Recent ethnic projections have showed white (and traditionally Christian) populations in the United States becoming a smaller and smaller percentage of the total population. That statistic indicates a strong growth of ethnic groups that have non-Christian elements. By the year 2050, one projection showed that white America will for the first time fall below the 50 percent level of total population. White America will no longer be a clear-cut majority of the population, although it will still be the largest of several minorities.[9]

This increase in minorities will mean growth for the world religions. Not only will the numbers of adherents of these religions grow, their percentages in terms of the total U.S. population will increase. As Gordon Melton has shown in his most recent edition of *The Encyclopedia of American Religions*, the diversity of denominations, both Christian and non-Christian, will continue to grow. More than

100 different Hindu denominations have been planted in America since 1965, and more than 75 forms of Buddhism currently exist.[10] Each of these communities now claims from three to five million adherents.

For Christians, this growth is a twofold challenge. First is a personal challenge. Living and getting along with neighbors of different religious traditions in a pluralistic society like America's is a unique and unfamiliar responsibility. We are told by neither church tradition nor by laws of religion how to act. How do I love my neighbor? What style of evangelism is appropriate for a free society? Where do being a good neighbor and a good Christian merge—and diverge?

Second is an institutional and political challenge. The Bible teaches, and recent events certainly support, the fact of continuing religious diversity in this world. Even if the next century of missions is the most successful we have ever had and we reach all the unreached peoples of the world with the gospel, there will still be millions who choose not to embrace Christianity. Indeed, the geographic mixing and fragmentation of other world religions will probably increase. Thus, the "this world is not my home" teaching of the New Testament will be put to the test.[11] We have lived comfortably with the assumption that our nation was predominantly and semiofficially Christian. But no longer. The United States will certainly not be so Christian a country as it has been. (Opinion on just how Christian a nation it has been varies, of course.)

Unfortunately, it is unlikely that all the interaction with people of other religions will be nice.[12] If history is any guide, there will be clashes similar to those clashes that the immigration of Hindus in the early decades of this century created, and that the influx of missionary-minded Muslims is creating today. People feel strongly about their religious traditions. It is unavoidable that confrontations will occur when those religious traditions postulate different answers to the most important questions of life: *Who am I? Who made me?* and *Where am I going?*

The United States has a good record of being able to incorporate dissent and difference. Our political system allows people to disagree strongly and yet pull together for overall goals. The political and institutional question is whether or not the United States, as it becomes more pluralistic in religious heritage and background, can absorb an increasing level of intense difference and still operate effectively.[13]

Getting along with a classmate who happens to be from India is entirely within the realm of possibility. One-to-one, the problem seems solvable. The problem, however, extends beyond interpersonal interaction with neighbors of different faiths. Our political and cultural stability—our way of life—*is* also at stake.

Chapter 3

COMPETING MISSIONARIES

The Metropolitan Museum of Modern Art in New York City has reigned majestically on the edge of Central Park for 110 years. Paintings and sculptures from all over the world adorn its walls and fill its alcoves. This museum testifies to man's unending quest for beauty in all its diversity.

Surrounding the Great Hall balcony, squeezed between the displays of Islamic art and ancient musical instruments, sits the Asian art section. Here from Indian jungles and Pakistani rice paddies sit ancient Hindu statues and paintings. One can stand in front of a black stone Vishnu flanked by consorts—a twelfth-century work from India. Moving down the hall, one can almost feel the jungle vines surrounding a tenth-century sandstone Shiva, or look beside it to a bronze dancing Shiva from Tamil Nadu. With imagination one can detect some of the passion of the artists as they created these sculptures.

In the staid setting of the New York Metropolitan Museum of Art, however, they seem sterile. Although hundreds of people are circulating in the halls, a strange quiet and calm hangs in the air. The commitment is to clean, thoughtful, neutral display.

The people looking at the statues and paintings are people at leisure. They are intellectual browsers, interested yet uninvolved, moved perhaps by the beauty of the works but uncommitted to them. They wear tiny white tin badges as proof that they paid their admission but proof also of their detachment.

In only ten minutes one can walk across Central Park to 34 West 71st Street, a three-story brownstone typical of early twentieth-century New York. But one may as well have walked halfway around the world when one compares the Hindu statues of the museum to the atmosphere in this building. A brass plate next to the door signals that here is the Vedanta Society, an organization dedicated to making the ancient teachings of the Hindu Vedas available to Westerners. It was founded in 1893 and has served a small but growing number of New Yorkers ever since. The difference between the museum and this brownstone becomes obvious the minute you open the door and walk in.

One immediately passes from a five-foot-square foyer to a long, narrow room with chairs for about 150 people. Thirty people, mostly seated toward the front, listen intently to the yellow-tunicked Swami Tathagatananda speak from a lectern at the right front corner. It is Sunday morning. If it were not for several distinguishing features of the room, one might think he had stumbled into a small house church in Manhattan.

In this room, however, the smell of incense is strong. In the front center is an altar where two candles and two bowls of flowers flank a large photo of Swami Vivekananda. A piano and two large sitars sit in the left front corner. The audience's attention is riveted on the lecture:

"The greatest help in life is meditation . . . you will find the Divine Light within . . . it's that light you must meditate on. Don't think of matter but on the Spirit within you."[1]

No white tin badges of neutrality here. As the swami lectures, the people in the chairs listen attentively. They are straining to catch the meaning behind the Indian's words. Their eyes flash with commitment and dedication. They are searching for a reason to be.

They include an Anglo man in a white cable knit sweater and white hair; a ponytailed housewife with a middle-aged husband in a brown suit; a black woman in a business outfit; an Indian woman with hair tightly pulled back in a bun, dark brown skin, colorful skirt, and black horn-rimmed glasses.

"It doesn't make any difference whether you're in Benares or Bethlehem or Mecca. Holiness is within you; the spirited place is within yourself."

On the wall is the Hindu Sanskrit figure for the sacred Om, the Christian cross, and the Muslim star and crescent. *The truth is one, men are called variously,* says the inscription underneath these signs. Swami Tathagatananda quotes from Augustine, the Gospel of John, the Qur'an, and many times from the Upanishads, the ancient Indian holy texts. Yet the illustrations are of modern New York: "Yesterday I saw an old homeless couple on the street. I see them on the street often. They have nowhere to go. Why? Their brain is not functioning. It's in a state of spiritual coldness."

After the service I talk to two Anglo men at the rear of the long room. There is a small library where Vedanta books are sold. I learn in talking to the men that there are fourteen such centers around America. No high pressure proselytizing here: "We like to let people find their own way. We supply them with literature and then hope they get interested."

I come away from my visit to the museum and the Hindu service with a clear sense of a change taking place in America. The kind of pluralism the museum represents—the cosmopolitan, worldly-wise knowledge that a big, strange world surrounds us all—has been with us for a long time. It is a pluralism easy to live with. The pluralism of the brownstone, however, is different altogether. The museum is detached, cool; the brownstone is intense and passionate. The museum asks for and expects no commitment; the brownstone, however low-key its methodology, exists to foster commitment. One offers information; the other seeks converts.

Technically, the presence of Hinduism (and other world religions) in this country is as old as the republic itself, or at least as old as the museums and libraries that have been here to display and describe them. But the temples, mosques, and other meeting halls and the "denominations" and institutions that support them are much more recent. They are growing in number, attendance, and power. They are rapidly becoming major competitors to Christianity.

Hinduism: Absorbing others

The initial impetus to mission-minded Hinduism in this country was the World Parliament of Religions at the Chicago World's Fair in 1893.[2] Religious figures from every major faith around the world came and spoke at the first world conference of major world faiths. The undisputed star of the show was a Hindu swami from India named Vivekananda. With flowing white hair highlighting his dark brown skin, he proved to be a master orator who held the conference spellbound with his common sense wisdom and message of peace for all mankind. His basic teaching was that our real nature is divine. God, the underlying reality, exists in every being. Religion is a search for self-knowledge, a search for the god within ourselves. We should not think of ourselves as needing to be "saved"; we are never lost. At worst, we are only living in ignorance of our true nature. That has been the message of the Vedanta Society in the United States for almost 100 years. After Swami Vivekananda cast his pearls before the attendees at the parliament, he went home to India a hero. They immediately sent him back with the encouragement to preach the word to all of America.[3]

Preaching to America: This adventure was novel for Hindus. Hinduism had never considered itself a missionary religion. In fact, in many ways Hinduism did not always consider itself a religion. The term *Hindu* embraces an incredible variety of religious practices in India and is closer to being a nationalistic or ethnic term than a designation for a specific corpus of beliefs. Self-contained as it always was in India, "Hinduism" never really felt the need to define itself, much less spread itself beyond its borders.

Two events changed this isolated insouciance. One was the Muslim invasions of the seventh and eighth centuries. Mission-minded Muslims from the Middle East swept across northern India leveling hundreds of Hindu and Buddhist temples and monasteries. For the first time in its existence, Hinduism faced an alien, threatening world view. The second event was the coming of the British in the sixteenth and seventeenth centuries—for with them came Christian missionaries. Both of these forces impelled Hindu scholars and thinkers to define more precisely what it was to be a Hindu as distinct from being a Muslim or a Christian.

Those challenges occasioned two reform movements in India. In the eighteenth century Ram Mohan Roy started an organization called the Brahmo Samaj. Roy adopted the Christian practice of regular congregational worship and rejected some features of old Hinduism, most notably idolatry, the caste system, and the sacrificial cult. Dayananda Sarasvati led a second reform movement in the nineteenth century called the Arya Samaj. Sarasvati preached a return to the original Vedic scriptures. He advocated a return to fundamentalist Hinduism.

These movements appealed to the ethnic and cultural instinct of the people and were quite successful. In the nineteenth century a charismatic figure, Ramakrishna, jumped on the reform bandwagon and founded the Ramakrishna Mission. He preached the ancient message of classical Hinduism (all religions are one) and attempted to incorporate the Christian and Muslim faiths as subsects of Hinduism. It was this message that Vivekananda took to America.

Thus *evangelism* in Hinduism is an ambivalent term. It does not mean trying to get someone to change religion. It means getting people to see that their religion is surely true but simply part of the bigger, worldwide religious picture. All religions are paths to the One Truth. Of course, Hinduism usually is seen as the purest path to the Truth because it is the one world religion that recognizes the truth and validity of all others.[4]

"Evangelistic" methods in Hinduism, then, tend toward absorption and abstraction. Like a giant amoeba, Hindu philosophy and thought tend to engulf everything that comes within its reach. By pushing the ideas of Truth and God and Spirit to their highest abstraction, one arrives at a homogenized view of religion that can indeed include almost everything in existence.[5]

In one form or another this monism has been quite successful in the United States. Often it is not associated at all with Hinduism but with fads or cults. The New Age movement is perhaps the prime current example.

Hinduism in its purer forms has also been quite successful. It was hard sledding in the early twentieth century when immigration laws forbade the entrance of Indians into the United States. For fifty years or so Hinduism was deprived of the prime ingredient for a foreign religious tradition to become entrenched: a committed immigrant population. After World War II, however, when the immigration laws were relaxed and Indians began to come to the United States in large numbers, temples and other centers of worship were built. Elaborate Hindu temples just like those one sees in Indian landscapes began to appear around the country. At first they were built mainly in large cities such as Pittsburgh, New York, and Chicago, but then they spread to more rural areas such as Nevada and Hawaii. Currently there are forty such temples. In 1937 the Indian League of America was formed on the East Coast to help raise the popular perceptions of Indian immigrants. Along with that perception came a new and grudging respect for the Hindu tradition itself. Today a number of Hindu organizations exist, some publishing newspapers (*Hinduism Today*, published in Hawaii, for example[6]), and others doing organizational and promotional work aimed at growth.

Buddhism: Adapting to the environment

In contrast to the low-key ambiance of the Manhattan Vedanta Service is the native urgency of a service at the Nichiren Shoshu Buddhist Temple of West Chicago, Illinois. One does not slip unobtrusively into a service. At the door of the temple, hostesses greet visitors and pointedly ask them if they are members—and if not, would they please sign a guest card. The service itself is anything but laid back. Electricity fills the air as rhythmic chanting forms the twenty-minute prologue to the service. Over and over the chant—*nam-myoho-renge-kyo*—fills the air as a huge gong at the front sounds out the beat.[7] The visitor, seated among six hundred people from all walks of life and all parts of Chicago, cannot help feeling caught up in the choreographed sound of commitment from members of this peculiar Japanese Buddhist sect.

The intensity is not a recent innovation, nor a Western marketing accommodation (although American Buddhists seem to have liberally borrowed from church-growth principles). No, Buddhism is one of the world's great missionary religions. On his death bed the Buddha himself sent out the first group of disciples to spread the new faith: "Go, monks, preach the noble doctrine. Let not two of you go into the same direction."[8] This text from the Pali canon of sacred Buddhist teachings shows both the missionary ideal that has inspired Buddhism from the earliest times, and the suggested methodology—individual efforts of itinerant monks and preachers. This charge helped spread Buddhism from its Indian roots to Sri Lanka, China, Tibet, and Japan, the four corners of the then-known world.

In order to achieve this kind of success Buddhism used a different strategy than the Hindu way of absorption. The Buddhist tradition relied on its adaptability and flexibility as it confronted widely divergent cultures. If the Hindu evangelistic totem is the amoeba, the Buddhist counterpart would be the chameleon. As a chameleon changes color to blend in with its environment, yet remains the same chameleon, Buddhists have been able to adapt their doctrines to different cultural settings without losing the essence of the teaching. In Sri Lanka, the Buddhist faith adapted to an animistic, literalistic, rationalistic mentality. In China, it merged with Confucianism and Taoism and provided an ideological superstructure on which to hang the ethical and naturalistic tenets of those two indigenous traditions. In Tibet, Buddhism molded itself to the desires of the ancient Bon tradition and became an esoteric, meditative, intuitive faith. And in Japan, it adapted itself nicely to the nationalistic Shinto religion of ancestor worship.

These adaptions were not haphazard accommodations. The basic core of Buddhist teaching survived. Indeed, the presence of an active World Buddhist Fellowship, coordinating all Buddhist sects in the world today, testifies to the fact that there is a core teaching that can clearly be called Buddhist. The cultural trappings, however, change radically from country to country.

For example, the Nichiren Shoshu service is obviously aimed at an American culture. The theme of the sermon is prosperity: meditation will make you happy and successful. It is the Buddhist version of the health-and-wealth gospel. It has obvious working-class appeal. Scattered throughout the audience in this suburban Chicago community are many poor urban blacks who have been bussed out from the inner city for the service. They are matched by an equal number of Japanese immigrants and perhaps 20 percent white suburbanites. The management and marketing techniques of American mass movements are obvious. In attempting to talk to the priests after the service, the visitor is immediately shuttled off to an office and given materials that explain the teaching and what further steps one must take to become more involved. In less than a week's time the visitor is invited to a private home for a "testimony" time with ten suburban Buddhists who have found great joy and peace in Nichiren Shoshu Buddhism.

The Buddhist community has grown quickly in America. Two visible signs of that maturity appeared in 1987. The first Buddhist chaplain was named to the armed forces, and an all-American Buddhist Congress was formed, an organization that will attempt to build a more adequate understanding of Buddhists and Buddhism in American society and be a voice for the Buddhist community's opinions on matters of public policy.[9] Clearly, Buddhists want to have a voice in American religion, politics, and culture to match the estimated four million Buddhists in this country. The Buddhist Church of America claims to have a hundred fairly large churches scattered throughout the United States.

The evidences of expanding Buddhist influence are apparent in the news: a story about Buddhist monks giving a drum performance in Carnegie Hall; a story about Vietnamese refugees and their Buddhist faith. The *Chronicle of Higher Education* runs a story on the Naropa Institute, a fully accredited liberal arts college in Boulder, Colorado, started by a Tibetan Buddhist guru, Chogyam Trungpa, in 1974. (It is successful and well known for its quality of education.) Major Theravada Buddhist *viharas* (temples) are in both Washington, D.C., and Los Angeles. One of our states, Hawaii, is predominantly Buddhist in religious orientation. Several major Buddhist umbrella organizations in the United States are aimed at unifying the various strands of Buddhism. The most prominent is the World Buddhist Association in Los Angeles.[10] It looks as though Buddhism is digging in for the long haul.

Islam: An uncompromising call

When it comes to missionary zeal, however, no one can match the Muslims. They call their mission *da'wah*, which literally means an invitation or a summoning. Muhammad used the word many times in the Qur'an, calling for believers to spread Islam:

Invite all to the Way of thy Lord with wisdom and beautiful preaching; and argue with them in ways that are best and most gracious. For thy Lord knoweth best who have strayed from his path and who receive guidance. And if ye do catch them out, catch them out no worse than they catch you out. But if ye show patience, that is indeed the best course.[11]

Early in their history the Muslims developed a comprehensive political theology aimed at spreading Islam worldwide. This theology included not only the domination of religious life of various Islamic countries (and non-Islamic countries, of course) but also domination of their political and economic life. Called *shari'a*, this political/economic/religious law covers every aspect of life, from banking laws to political structures to religious life to personal ethics. *Da'wah* is the preaching of the Muslim way of life, including *shari'a* law.

Public relations–minded Muslims point out that sometimes *da'wah* is confused with the Islamic teaching of *jihad* or holy war. *Da'wah's* mission, they say, should never be spread by force. If the hearers refuse to embrace Islam, then they should be left alone. But a committed Muslim should never give up. If nothing else succeeds, at least God may use a silent example of a model Muslim as a means to someone's conversion.

Evidence in the Qur'an, however, indicates that occasionally *jihad*, or the use of force, is reasonable. Sura 2 says to "fight them on until there is no more tumult or oppression and there prevail justice and faith in God. But if they cease, let there be no hostility except to those who practice oppression."[12]

Sometimes the spiritual and moral aspects of *jihad* are emphasized. Muhammad himself once said, "We have now returned from the lesser *jihad* (that is, fighting) to the greater *jihad.*" Rudolph Peters has noted about *jihad* and its uses in the Qur'an: "Careful reading of the qur'anic passages on *jihad* suggests that Muhammad regarded the command to fight the unbelievers not as absolute but as conditional upon provocation from them. In many places this command is justified by perfidy on the part of the non-Muslims."[13]

Since the Qur'an appears to have conflicting passages on the doctrine of *jihad*, the interpreters of the doctrine are many. At the very least, one can say that *da'wah* and *jihad* together form an extremely strong motivation for converting others to the Islamic faith.

Within a century of Muhammad's founding of Islam, this strong urge to spread the faith had resulted in the conversion of all of northern Africa, from Saudi Arabia to the Atlantic Ocean. Islam spread across the Mediterranean into Spain. Had Charles Martel not defeated the Muslim armies at the Battle of Tours in 732, Islam would have spread over all of Europe.[14] Islam also spread east and north of Saudi Arabia. In fact, the Muslim capture of Israel and the Holy Land was the occasion of the seven Christian crusades in the eleventh, twelfth, and thirteenth centuries.

In Islam, the emphasis on conversion is uncompromising and intense. Islam is a simple faith summed up in the single phrase "There is no God but Allah and Muhammad is his prophet." Anyone who can assent to that is a Muslim; anyone who cannot is not.[15] Thus, the missionary endeavor tends to be a black-and-white affair: Take it or leave it. There is no attempt at inclusiveness, and certainly no attempt at relativizing or adapting the faith. Rather than the amoeba or chameleon, the animal that best represents Islamic missions is the tiger.

Fortunately, the sword is not used in America to convert; still, the efforts at evangelization are strong. Not too long ago in Hanover Park, Illinois, a typical effort played itself out in the recreation room of a neighborhood community center. Upon entering the room, one might imagine oneself in a church basement: folding tables covered with white butcher paper; linoleum floors; one table full of fried chicken, potato salad, and a steaming pot of green beans. It was a church-basement supper all over. But at this supper, the program was not a homily from the Gospels but a reading from the Qur'an. The audience was about two hundred people. One hundred were Middle Eastern immigrant Muslims; the other one hundred were white Chicago suburbanites invited to the meeting by the immigrants, who had met them at work. The pitch was not hard sell. But it was definite. Common ground was established: the mutual concerns of both Christians and Muslims for morality. The immoral use of drugs, alcohol, and sex are as taboo in Islam as they are in conservative Christianity. The evidence that these kinds of meetings are successful is not apparent yet, but that certainly is not because these approaches are not tried.

Kent Hart reports in an article in Fuller Theological Seminary's *Theology News and Notes* that since 1981, Muslims have been increasingly encouraged to invite Americans to the truth of Islam. He notes that the major Muslim organizations state this as one of their four principal goals.[16]

American Muslims receive outside help. The Muslim World League, founded in 1962 in Mecca, assists Islamic causes throughout the world. It distributes free English translations of the Qur'an and other Islamic literature and thus supports Islamic missionary activity. It provides *imams* (preachers) for American mosques. In 1981 it gave more than a half-million dollars to sixteen mosques in the United States.

What's new?

What is new in evangelism in each of these world religions is the difference between the museum and the church. In one form or another, the world with its esoteric and ancient religions has always been with us. But it has never been with us in such an immediate and competitive way. Hinduism, Buddhism, and Islam are no longer traditions our children read about in textbooks: They may now experience them in everyday life—at school, in the newspapers, in churches, temples, and mosques.

Institutions of the major world religions hold "Bible" studies for nonadherents (in this case, Upanishad, Dharma studies), they have elaborate "Sunday school" curriculum for children of all ages, and they have evening "church" suppers at which they teach the tenets of their faith to neighborhood Christians.[17] Although they are already protected by law, they actively lobby legislators and influence judges to make more specific rulings in favor of Hindu, Buddhist, and Muslim freedoms. They witness at work, and they are involved in social action programs.

Those programs are not ineffective. Daron Goodson, a mechanical engineering student at Howard University in Washington, D.C., remembers the first night he came in contact with the Islamic faith. "A friend invited me to go to a talk about this new religion. I went, and I heard readings from the Qur'an. It seemed logical and clear. I was raised a Christian, but Christianity didn't seem to have the answers to the crime and injustices I saw on the streets of Washington. That night I recognized that the one true God is Allah and Muhammad was his prophet." Daron changed his name to Abu Bakr (Father of the Camel, the name of the first caliph) and began attending the Islamic Center in Washington. "Now I don't have this feeling (that I used to have with Christianity) that everyone is making up their own rules. Islam is logical. It is the truth."

The question facing Christians is not whether we can avoid the competition. We can't. The real question is how to enter into that competition fairly and effectively. Perhaps the question is even deeper. How can this competition be carried out *Christianly?* What are the bedrock issues involved? What are the questions that must be answered in order to remain true to the Christian Great Commission to spread the gospel to all the people in the world?

Chapter 4

PLURALISM 101

The winter of 1989 will long be remembered for striking the fear of Allah into writers' hearts. Iran's Ayatollah Khomeini hung a death sentence on Indian author Salman Rushdie for *The Satanic Verses*, a book he claimed blasphemed the prophet Muhammad. Protests over the book in Pakistan, Iran, Belgium, and the United States were intense. In Pakistan, where the protests were as much political as religious, rioters were killed.

Rushdie, a resident of Great Britain, went into hiding. The sales of his otherwise mediocre novel rocketed, reaching the top of several worldwide lists, including the *New York Times*, where it remained for several weeks. The protest was bloody and ineffective.

The contrast is startling between Rushdie's plight and that of Martin Scorsese, writer and director of the movie *The Last Tempta-*

tion of Christ. The summer before the Rushdie affair, Universal Pictures released Scorsese's film version of Jesus' life—a depiction that many Christians found blasphemous. They demonstrated in front of theaters, wrote letters by the ream, and boycotted several of Universal's other productions. Although the initial publicity probably helped promote the mediocre film, the protests got their point across: the film was objectionable, having little relationship to the life of Jesus that the Bible portrays. Christians had their peaceful say, and life—everyone's life—went on.

In both cases, a religious point of view created controversy as it offended religious people. There was, however, a vast difference in the way religious ideas competed. The contrast makes one lesson clear: Religious freedom works. Although the political system America uses is not perfect, in cases similar to the Rushdie and Scorsese affairs it has, time after time, proved superior to others. Elsewhere in the world, religion is controlled to fit state purposes; America crafts laws to make religious freedom even freer. While other nations deny dissent, our nation encourages it. Others attempt to legislate lifelong faithfulness to one tradition; in America, changing churches (or temples?) is common. The result is religious diversity, which sometimes brings confusion and error. But more important, believers feel secure that they can practice their faith in safety.

This situation prompts two major questions: How did the United States get its ethic of toleration? Will it continue to work in an increasingly pluralistic culture?

A unique system

The legal framework for religion in the United States is based on just a few sentences in the nation's founding documents,[1] principally the First Amendment: "Congress shall make no law respecting an establishment of religion, or prohibiting the free exercise thereof."

Two guarantees are here that, held in tension, provide religious freedom: the government will not insist on one religion (or any religion), but the government will protect individuals as they practice whatever religion they choose. This "protective-indulgent parent" role that our government plays has worked.

There are, however, conditions that allow it to work.[2] It assumes a common moral core that defines what "acceptable" religion is. The United States government does draw the line, for example, at endorsing ancient Aztec Indian religion of human sacrifice. But this moral core, what C. S. Lewis called the "tao,"[3] easily accommodates the world's major religions.

Several other statements reinforce and explain further the protections of the First Amendment. One is from the Declaration of Independence: "We hold these truths to be self-evident, that all men are created equal, that they are endowed by their Creator with certain unalienable Rights, that among these are Life, Liberty and the pursuit of Happiness." The other is from the Constitution: "No religious Test shall ever be required as a Qualification to any Office or public Trust under the United States."

The roots of these statements are European. Although the British did not have religious freedom as it came to be defined in the United States, certain British documents paved the way for the American position. The Magna Charta of 1215, for example, said "the Church of England shall be free, and enjoy her whole rights and liberties inviolate."

Of all the U.S. Presidents, Abraham Lincoln most expanded the principle of religious freedom. On March 30, 1863, he proclaimed a National Day of Humiliation, Fasting, and Prayer, with the following words, "It is the duty of nations as well as of men to own their dependence upon the overruling power of God to confess their sins and transgressions in humble sorrow. Yet with assured hope that genuine repentance will lead to mercy and pardon and to recognize the sublime truth announced in the Holy Scriptures and proved by all history that those nations only are blessed whose God is the Lord." Theodore Roosevelt later added, "in this happy country of ours, religion and liberty are natural allies."

Practically, those commitments to religious freedom have had the following effects:

● No one ever has second thoughts about starting a new church for fear of government interference;

● People change churches and religions without giving legality a second thought; only their consciences and perhaps some sociological factors need be considered;

● Religious freedom has encouraged an incredible diversity of religions and, within Christianity, denominations; there are literally hundreds of each;

- Freedom has allowed religious competition with a bare minimum of rancor and almost no violence;
- Freedom has allowed religion to play a spiritual and ethical role as society's conscience, constructively criticizing political, economic, and cultural affairs.

To the rest of the world, this kind of freedom has been little short of astounding. An early French visitor to our shores, Alexis de Tocqueville, could not get over it:

"The religious atmosphere of the country was the first thing that struck me on arrival in the United States. The longer I stayed in the country the more conscious I became of the important political consequences resulting from the novel situation. . . . My longing to understand the reason for this phenomenon increased daily. To find this out, I questioned the faithful of all communions; I particularly sought the society of clergymen, who are the depositories of the various creeds and have a personal interest in their survival. . . . I expressed my astonishment and revealed my doubts to each of them; I found that they all agreed with each other except about details; all thought that the main reason for the quiet sway of religion over their country was the complete separation of church and state."[4]

De Tocqueville and others were astounded that religion without the apparent support of state endorsement could be so vigorous: "I wondered how it could come about that by diminishing the apparent power of religion it increased its real strength. . . . When a religion seeks to found its sway only in the longing for immortality equally tormenting every human, it can aspire to universality; but when it comes to uniting itself with a government, it must adopt maxims which apply only to certain nations. Therefore, by allying itself with any political power religion increases its strength over some but forfeits the hope of reigning over all."[5]

Unique history
One has to go all the way back to a third century B.C. Buddhist monarchy in India, King Asoka's, to find anything like what we see in the U.S. Constitution. India in Asoka's time was an amalgamation

of feudal kingdoms. Asoka managed to consolidate many of those kingdoms together under his rule. He did it through encouraging Buddhist missions, but also by recognizing the basic human right to a free conscience. He made his policies known to his subjects by having them carved on conspicuously placed rocks at strategic points of the kingdom. On one of these rock inscriptions he decreed:

"King Priyadarsi [Asoka] wishes members of all faiths to live everywhere in his kingdom for they all seek mastery of the senses and purity of mind. Men are different in their inclinations and passions, however, and they may perform the whole of their duties or only part. Even if one is not able to make lavish gifts, mastery of the senses, purity of mind, gratitude and steadfast devotion are commendable and essential. King Priyadarsi honors men of all faiths, members of religious orders and laymen alike with gifts and various marks of esteem yet he does not value either gifts or honors as much as growth and the qualities essential to religion in men of all faiths.

"This growth may take many forms but its fruit is in guarding one's speech to extolling one's own faith and disparaging the faith of others inappropriately or when the occasion is appropriate immoderately.

"The faiths of others all deserve to be honored for one reason or another. By honoring them, one exalts one's own faith and at the same time performs a service to the faith of others. By acting otherwise one injures one's own faith and also does disservice to others for if a man extols his own faith and disparages another because of devotion to his own and because he wants to glorify it, he seriously injures his own faith.

"Therefore, concord alone is commendable for through concord men may learn and respect the conception of Dharma [that is, the divine law] accepted by others. King Priyadarsi desires men of all faiths to know each other's doctrines and to acquire sound doctrines. Those who are attached to their particular faiths should be told that King Priyadarsi does not value gifts or honors as much as growth in the qualities essential to religion and men of all faiths.

"Many officials are assigned to tasks bearing on this purpose—the officers in charge of spreading Dharma, the superintendents of women in the royal household, the inspectors of cattle and pasture-lands, and other officials.

"The objective of these measures is the promotion of each man's particular faith and the glorification of Dharma."[6]

Between Asoka and the writing of the United States Constitution in the eighteenth century, however, religion found itself inevitably subservient to, master of, or in competition with the government of the day. Even in Christianity the concept of religious freedom and separation of church and state was nonexistent.[7]

A historical overview

No status, 30–312. For the first three hundred years of its existence, Christianity's Middle Eastern, North African, Greek, and Roman hosts viewed Christianity as a dangerous cult—if they gave it any thought at all. A cynic could call this complete separation of church and state. But that implies that the church had enough status to be considered an entity over against the government. In truth, it did not. Christianity was viewed with the same jaundiced eye we would cast today on that strange, hippie commune in the big house down the street. Christians were seen with suspicion and distrust.

Imperial domination, 312–590. Several factors brought about gradual change. For one, Christians proved to be good neighbors. They caused little trouble, took care of one another, and even helped the non-Christian poor. In some parts of the empire, Christians adopted the practice of burying the disenfranchised dead who would otherwise be left to rot in the open air. Romans noticed, and in 311 the Emperor Galerius issued a decree of toleration for Christians. Two years later a new emperor, Constantine, adopted Christianity as his own faith and declared it the religion of the empire. This declaration made the church a ward of the state with all the privileges—and dangers—of being the favorite son. On the positive side of the ledger, official sanction allowed the church to spread even more rapidly throughout the Roman Empire. On the negative side, Constantine used the church to further his political ends: A common religious faith is a good tool for unifying groups of people.

Church-state alliance. A great advance in church-state relations occurred when Augustine wrote a book called *The City of God*. From his North African bishopric across the Mediterranean Sea, Augustine watched in horror as wave after wave of European Vandals and Goths took turns sacking the once-invincible Rome. Refugees from Italy fled to North Africa. Augustine heard Christians among them asking this question: *What is to become of the church now that Rome has fallen?* Augustine realized the danger of the church being so closely tied to the state that its fortunes could rise and fall with the political winds. But Augustine was also a practical leader of men and knew that a relationship was inevitable between "the city of God" and "the city of man." His solution was an alliance that worked well in the fifth and sixth centuries, with the pope and the emperor coequals in different realms.

Church domination, 590–1517. When the Roman Empire finally and completely broke up, the church was faced with a new world order. The situation was roughly this: People still longed for centralized authority to protect them, something Rome could no longer provide. Because the church's structures were still in place, people looked to the church for unifying authority. The popes were happy to oblige.

Thus, during the Middle Ages the church became the authority to reckon with in Europe. In Italy, things developed further. The Papal States, formed toward the end of the Middle Ages, amounted to ecclesiastical governments run by the various popes.

State churches, 1512–1776. The Reformers reacted against what they perceived as ecclesiastical tyranny. They particularly objected in principle to papal authority. Calvin and Luther, however, adopted different strategies; on the one hand, Calvin structured the government of Geneva on the principle of the church still having a strong role vis-à-vis the state; on the other hand, Martin Luther did not think that Rome should dominate, but neither did he adopt the papal state/Calvinistic approach that the church should determine what the state does. For Luther, the roles of these two institutions would be intolerably confused. Luther endorsed the state and church ruling their respective spheres, the temporal and the spiritual. Because the state provided order and protection for all, to some extent the state provided order and protection for the churches as well. National state churches resulted and are still common in much of Europe. In England, after a turbulent period of alternating

Roman and national allegiances, the Church of England settled into a reasonably quiet existence following the Act of Uniformity, 1662. Scotland has its Presbyterian Church, Sweden its Lutheran Church, and some of the Balkan States have Eastern Orthodox Churches.

This plan did not prove to be wholly acceptable, however, because it gave the religious nod to one particular group and made it very difficult for other groups to exist. Groups that objected most vociferously and with the most success were the Puritans and other Calvinistic separatists in England. The Puritans objected to Elizabeth I's compromise vision for the Church of England, a political settlement halfway between Rome and Reform. Later, the Puritans even gained control of the English Parliament for a short period. They proved, however, unequal to the task of establishing an adequate system for recognizing the pluralistic concerns of state and sectarian religious groups. That feat was left to the American experiment to work out.

Some groups of Puritans, other Calvinistic separatists, and Anabaptists immigrated to the United States and earned a second opportunity to influence religious freedom. Although the Puritans believed the church should judge the state, a position the United States would not adopt, Puritans did influence the idea of an autonomous church. It was left to some heirs of the European Anabaptist movement (notably Isaac Backus) to be most influential in injecting the idea of the complete separation of church and state.

The U.S. doctrine of separation of church and state was created within this milieu of European immigrant Christianity. All of the basic documents of early America reflect Christian thought. The Liberty Bell is inscribed with a passage from Leviticus 25:10: "Proclaim liberty throughout the land unto all the inhabitants thereof." A frequently quoted passage in the early documents was Mark 12:14–17, where some Pharisees, attempting to trip up Jesus, asked him, "Is it lawful to give tribute to Caesar or not?" Jesus answered wisely: "Render to Caesar the things that are Caesar's, and to God the things that are God's." These verses were used to describe the American philosophy toward the respective roles of religion and government.

When the founders of our country talked about religious freedom, they were talking about *Christian* religious freedom. Benjamin

Franklin, George Washington, John Adams, Thomas Jefferson, James Madison, Alexander Hamilton, Samuel Adams, and John Jay were all, at least in name, Christians. Their intent was that different Christian denominations and sects should have religious freedom. Whether they included the world religions (even Judaism) is unlikely.[8]

The language in which they wrote the official state documents, however, in no way restricts religious freedom to *Christian* religious freedom. Providentially, many think, they wrote documents that have the capacity to incorporate our modern pluralistic setting. Today, with the growing presence of world religions in the United States, the ethic of religious freedom extends beyond an essentially Christian culture. In our context, religious freedom is more crucial than ever.

Enjoyed, but never tested
In sum, the situation is this:
1. All of the founding documents were based on Christian principles;
2. The founders themselves were at least nominally Christian;
3. The founders probably assumed Christianity would always be dominant;
4. Christianity is not dominant now, and it is left to us to tease out the implications of religious freedom in a religiously plural culture.

Forty years ago this pressure did not exist. The country remained nominally Christian and, in fact, nominally Protestant. Look at the church-state problems our country and its law courts dealt with around 1950: Jewish immigration, anti-Semitism, anti-Catholic bias and the Ku Klux Klan, the rise of the Roman Catholic Church, the teaching of evolution in the public schools, aggressive Jehovah's Witnesses, birth control and divorce laws, and pacifism. Some of these issues are still problems today, but to them we have added a long list of new problems: the presence of Islamic minarets on mosques; Muslim's right to call people to prayers over loudspeakers; Hindu temples and existing zoning laws; Buddhist chaplains in the armed forces; Friday holy days for Muslims in the workplace; and Hare Krishna devotees proselytizing in airport terminals.

However, even in the fifties a change had begun. Up until then, the metaphor used to describe the ethnic diversity of the United States was that of a melting pot. Elaborate, largely accurate schemes were suggested about how first- second- and third-generation ethnics slowly but surely assimilated themselves into the culture.[9] In the fifties and sixties, however, the image of roots replaced the melting pot image. Overwhelmed with the increased pluralism of society, people looked longingly for anything that would give them identity in an increasingly impersonal world. Ethnic pride for many became more important than adjusting to the American scene. People longed to be a little different rather than to melt into the American Pot. The Jewish American discussions of Zionism, and later the black consciousness movements, had prepared the ground for this new national metaphor. Serious questions about the limits of assimilation gave rise to questions about how to cope with a more-or-less permanent pluralism. In short, the problem shifted from *How can I become more like my neighbors?* to *How can neighbors so different from one another live together?*

Nowhere was this shift more evident than in the courts, both federal and state. The laws, of course, defended religious pluralism. But never before had so many really different religious people asked for protection under them. The courts obliged. Different Sabbaths, different clothing, different church requirements—all received court protection.

The strain of this diversity created a variety of responses. For the first time, some raised serious questions about the limits of religious freedom. Even some conservative Christians, the bedrock supporters of church-state separation, challenged the idea. One group, called Christian reconstructionists, or theonomists, argued for a country governed by Old Testament principles. Others have argued for more moderate means of maintaining their Christian majority—by sharply restricting immigration, for example. Of course, the extremists are always with us: white supremacists, extolling a poisonous brew of fundamental Christian beliefs and violent racism, have sprung up in various parts of the country.

Most Christians, however, still believe we have an adequate *political* system. The lessons of twentieth-century experiments with totalitarianism in Asia, Africa, and Eastern Europe have convincingly demonstrated the bankruptcy of state- (or church-) mandated uniformity. It doesn't work. Even after the annihilation of millions of lives of dissenters to achieve the ends of dictatorial schemes (of Stalin, Hitler, Pol Pot, etc.), totalitarian governments fail in the end. The democratic system and the separation of church and state is the genius of the United States system. It needs to be retained even in the face of religious pluralism.

Yet there are limits to how much pluralism can be accommodated while allowing the government to protect the common good. Some sense of community, some sense of being part of a larger whole that is more than the sum of its parts, is required to make democracy work. The freedom of religion cannot be an absolute.

On the other hand, we must avoid the temptations to restrict religion through a glorified secularism. Religious sentiments, with their emphases on values, morality, and ethics, are essential for democracy to work. Our problems with pluralism would not be solved if we could keep religion a strictly private matter, restricted to the home and the pew. Then even democracy would not work.

But if we avoid these two extremes, we have the best system for our shrinking, religiously plural world.

The bigger question comes from the other direction. Do we have an adequate *theology*, designed to meet the pressures of religious pluralism? We must now turn to that question.

Chapter 5

THE PROBLEM OF TRANSFORMING THE WORLD

In fashioning a theological approach toward the world religions, we must deal with two uniquenesses. One is a unique political situation, the other a unique gospel.

As we saw in chapter 4, our unique political situation guarantees freedom of religion to all. Political situations change, of course, and there are many parts of the world where religious freedom is not a fact of life. In the United States, however, we are free to worship (or not to worship) as we please. Most of us feel comfortable embracing that fact. We must develop our theology of pluralism with that factor in mind.

Our second uniqueness is the gospel of Jesus Christ. He is, we believe, more than just one of several pathways to God. He is the only way. And he is a timeless way: He is the same yesterday, today, and tomorrow. Whereas political systems change, the gospel never does. It is unique and unchanging.

"Doing theology" is nothing more than showing how the unchanging principles of the gospel apply to the changing politics (and cultures, economics, etc.) of the world. In order to address the challenge of twenty-first-century America, we must show what the gospel has to say to the religiously diverse, legally endorsed pluralism of our day.

We have many resources to draw upon, including a 2,000-year theological heritage and, more important, the teachings of Scripture. But before we look at those elements, we need to get clear in our minds just what it is that Christians attempt to do as they work and live and breathe the air of this exciting day and age.

Our attitude toward the world

Thirty years ago, H. Richard Niebuhr wrote a book called *Christ and Culture* in which he outlined five different ways Christians could relate to the world and its culture.[1] The book is still useful. Niebuhr's five options were: (1) Set faith *against* culture, a posture that leads to separation; (2) *Identify* Christian faith and culture as one and the same thing, a posture that leads to liberalism; (3) Set Christianity and culture in a hierarchical, philosophical *harmony*, a view typified by Thomas Aquinas and traditional Roman Catholic theology; (4) Separate the *spheres of influence* of Christ and culture, assigning to each specific roles in our fallen world; (5) View culture as a result of a degenerate, fallen creation and Christianity as a *transforming* agent trying to win back, inch by inch, the lost terrain.

Niebuhr recognized the valuable contribution of each of these positions, articulated by the greatest minds of church history. But he also recognized that "the great central tradition of the church" is the transforming model.[2] Historically, Christians have seen themselves as engaged in a desperate battle to change a world that has gone drastically wrong.

In determining the theologically correct stance to take vis-à-vis the world's religions, we need to make a similar *a priori* determination of just what it is we are seeking to do. If religious beliefs are defined as the answers to the ultimate questions of life, then once we have determined what these answers are, everything else we do in life needs to be ordered by them.

The Christian's answer to the question *What is life all about?* is this: Life should be lived as a mad scramble to restore a positive relationship with God and his created beings (us), a relationship that was destroyed by man's willful sin.

Everything we do, then, should be aimed at restoring and deepening our personal relationship with God and with helping others do the same.

Transform is the right word to use to describe this overriding purpose. The most famous scriptural use of this word sets transforming over against its polar opposite, *conforming.* "Do not conform any longer to the pattern of this world," Paul said, "but be transformed...."[3] As individual Christians are themselves transformed, they can go about the business of changing the world by making disciples in every corner of it. Don't let the world change you; don't be neutral to the world; don't separate yourself from the world. But let God transform you—and then, through you, the world.

Nothing characterizes the evangelical Christian more than this fundamental attitude of seeing ourselves as agents of God's transforming power.

The question then becomes *how* one takes the unchangeable, unique gospel and applies it to the ever-changing political and cultural situation. It is that *how* in the light of our unique political situation that needs to be addressed.

As we saw in the last chapter, our situation is unique, and the tremendous influx of world religions into this unique political situation is less than a half-century old. Thus, it is not surprising that the subtleties of this *how* have never been drawn out of Scripture by the great theologians. They had their own situations to address, and address them they did.

Although none of them had our unique church-state situation, it is still instructive to do a brief, selective, impressionistic survey of how they addressed the situations of their day and age.

Our theological heritage

Augustine, the great North African theologian, did his work as the Roman Empire was falling. He watched from across the Mediterranean Sea as Alaric and the Visigoths sacked Rome in 410. And then, even as Augustine himself was dying, the Vandals were at the gates of his beloved town of Hippo. They were all pagans, outside the pale of the church (although many had been converted to a heretical, Arian form of Christianity). Augustine had no personal contact with them, but throughout his life he devoted considerable energy to dealing with heretics such as the Donatists and the Pelagians, or to combating the dualism preached by the group that had attracted him as a youth, the Manichaeans. He was no stranger to religious pluralism.

Augustine developed several theological principles that remain crucial to our considerations. One is the concept of original sin, which he preached with great fervor. Another is the concept of the imperfect church, with the wheat and the tares growing together only to be sorted out by God at the end of history. These two doctrines—that all people are sinners, and that unbelievers will inevitably be found inside as well as outside the institutional church—help keep us from arrogance or utopianism as we deal with those of other faiths. "Everyone needs to be saved, but not everyone will be saved—even within the walls of the church." This singular message is an invitation to both missions and humility.[4] It helps us see the desperate need of the world apart from Christ without losing sight of the church's own faultiness.

Thomas Aquinas, the great Latin theologian of the thirteenth century, added an equally important element. Aquinas's contribution was his adamant conviction that human reason was trustworthy as long as it was placed under the protective and corrective umbrella of God's providence. It was this conviction (what G. K. Chesterton called Aquinas's belief in "organized common sense") that opened Christians to truth wherever it might be found. It ensured that Paul's teaching in Romans regarding general revelation was not consigned to the dustbin of Christian idealism. On the other hand, it probably suggested to some the possibility of salvation through other faiths. Aquinas was careful to say that although the pagans of classical antiquity could surely be saved through faith and divine providence, by the time of the Christian era no one could achieve salvation outside the ecclesiastical structures.

Aquinas was also the first theologian to confront the "threat" of a world religion. Islam had swept across North Africa and was moving up through southern Spain toward Europe. One of Islam's principal thinkers, Averroës, was doing for Islam what Aquinas was doing for Christianity. They were sanitizing the "pagan" Aristotle and utilizing him for both Christian and Muslim theology. Aquinas was ready to meet Averroës's challenge.

What is interesting about Aquinas's confrontation was his attitude. It was not one of denunciation but of correction. Ever the philosopher and theologian, he simply pointed out, step-by-step and in great detail, where Averroës was wrong in his interpretation of Aristotle. It was the same kind of attitude Aquinas took in writing the *Summa Contra Gentiles*, a four-volume work for Dominican missionaries in North Africa on how to convert unbelievers and heretics. Aquinas lived and died by the pen of reason rather than by the sword of war.[5]

One suspects that Martin Luther tended more toward the sword of war. Perhaps it is better to say that he treated his pen as a sword rather than an instrument of reasoned persuasion. His statements in the sixteenth century against the Turkish Muslims are some of the strongest ever written by a Christian theologian. In his treatise "On War Against the Turk," he said: "The Turk is the . . . servant of the raging devil. . . . If the Turk's god, the devil, is not beaten, there is reason to believe that the Turk will not be so easy to beat. . . . Muhammad commands that ruling is to be done by the sword . . . thus the Turk is nothing but a murderer or a highwayman."[6]

It is difficult to put a good face on Luther's comments and suggest that his statement is a contribution to our modern needs. It is probably better to look to Luther's renewed emphasis on Holy Scripture, and his recognition that salvation is a personal affair between God and man rather than man and the church. It is these latter two contributions that really serve us well today, making possible positive personal interaction with friendly non-Christians. Institutional interaction will inevitably be more cautious and less creative than the personal relationship possible between individuals of deep religious persuasions. Luther's emphasis on the priesthood of the believer made it possible for any Christian to see himself as God's representative to a needy world, without necessarily involving the church institutionally.

One looks in vain for any extended treatment of "pagans" in Calvin's voluminous writings—a significant fact as we consider contributions from our theological heritage. From the Reformation onward, Christian theologians gave little thought to the religious challenges from outside the Christian West. Calvin's real interest was in Geneva, among believers. He wanted to set up structures that would allow church and state to work hand in hand to create a Christian society. He accepted Augustine's dictum that fellowship with God is man's goal, and Luther's great teaching that salvation comes by grace alone through faith. Further, he was a remarkably humble man given his great intellectual and administrative skills. At one point he noted that even the best theology is only 80 percent correct. He still came down hard on those who "think that any zeal for religion however preposterous is sufficient."

Perhaps it is in the area of administration that Calvin made his greatest contribution to interfaith interaction. In Geneva he created a unique, adaptable, and efficient church organization, placing more emphasis on local church authority than anyone before him. This emphasis created flexible congregations that could adapt themselves to local conditions. This kind of church structure has borne great fruit, particularly in the American setting where remarkably resilient denominations and independent churches are able to survive the failures of denominational mistakes and the personal peccadilloes of unholy leaders. This adaptable church structure has created groups of believers that are more flexible and less threatened by other religions.

The two great theologians of America's early revivalistic religion, John Wesley and Jonathan Edwards, seemed blithely unaware of the larger arena of world religions. Both were concerned with reforming and rejuvenating their existing Christian tradition, and both were remarkably successful at doing so—Wesley with the Anglican church and the eventual creation of the Methodist church, and Edwards with his Puritan and Congregational connections. Wesley claimed that he "looked on all the world as his parish." But one has the distinct feeling that his parish did not extend far beyond traditional boundaries.

In our own century, Karl Barth spoke specifically to other religions, though he did so while questioning the status of religion itself, including Christianity. As the European church kowtowed more and more to Adolf Hitler's demands, Barth became less and less convinced that religion of any kind was a good idea. Like the great Reformers before him, Barth recognized that Christianity depends not on churches but on the person of Jesus Christ. In the tradition of Augustine and Calvin he called the church back to the Bible in an unswerving devotion to Jesus Christ. "Religion is unbelief. . . . It is a human attempt to anticipate what God in his revelation wills to do and does do." As such, religion, including Christianity, is a usurper of God's prerogative.

Barth warned against seeking a point of contact in other religions. He warned against any kind of accommodation with them. For Barth it was an either/or situation: One accepted Jesus Christ or one accepted religion; one could not accept both. Why, then, Barth was asked, is Christianity the true religion? Not because of what it is, he answered, but because God chose it to be. It is for that reason and that reason alone that Christianity is the one true faith.

Barth mentioned other religions in his famous paragraph 17 in Volume 1 of his *Church Dogmatics.*[8] He noted the similarities, for example, of Amida Buddhism and Bhakti Hinduism with certain aspects of Christian faith. However, Barth was adamant that no one should mistake these religious "truths" for any kind of general revelatory truth. Human beings cannot figure things out for themselves. Human knowledge is limited and historically conditioned. Let God be God. We must admit God's self-revelation in Jesus and quit trying to figure things out for ourselves.

Many think Barth went too far in centering everything on the Christ event. (For example, his doctrine of Scripture suffered.) Yet it is in some sense because of Barth that the uniqueness of Christ has become the chief rallying point for conservative Christians when they consider world religions. Liberal Christians often emphasize the common ground between Christianity and other world religions. Barth, however, put the focus on Christ as Lord.

Thus, we find ourselves with a tremendously fruitful heritage from the great theologians of church history. We know the humility of sin and an imperfect church, and the exclusivity of salvation in the unique person of Jesus Christ. We do not have the onerous burden of an excessive church hierarchy, or a distant God we cannot deal with. With these tools, plus the principles of Old Testament and New Testament interaction with other faiths, we have the equipment to develop a theology of pluralism.

What does the Bible say?

The Bible is no stranger to religiously plural situations. Both the Old and the New Testament are full of "biblical pluralisms," stories of what happens when the people of God—either the Old Testament Israelites or the New Testament church—clash with people of radically different world views. Approximately 138 such clashes are recorded in Scripture. The Bible is also full of teachings about how to behave toward unbelievers. Approximately 106 passages contain some kind of teaching relating to this problem.[9] We can learn a great deal from studying these 244 passages, searching for principles that will guide us today in our relationships with people of other faiths.

Of course, the task is not easy. We must take many variables into account. For example, what is the nature of the world view the people of God encountered? Of the 138 biblical clashes, 30 percent were with Greek and Roman religions, 25 percent with Canaanite religions, 10 percent each with Mesopotamian and Nabatean religions, and 5 percent with Egyptian religion. The other 20 percent were clashes with religiously undefined or atheistic groups.

A second variable: What was the political and religious situation for God's people in relation to other peoples and religions? If we are to learn from the 244 biblical pluralisms, we must always take these religio-political situations into account. In the Old Testament there are four different situations:

1. *Henotheism* was a tribal political situation in which every people had their own god, though they accepted the existence of other people's gods. This situation meant that some tribes chose the one true God from a whole menu of gods. He was *their* God—just as, for other tribes, another god was *their* god.

2. God (Yahweh) called one of these peoples to be his chosen people. They acted—politically, religiously, economically, culturally—in his name. This *theocracy* totally blurred the distinction between church and state, which today we find so comforting. It also left no doubt that Yahweh was the only real God over the whole earth—not just over his people.

3. God's people wanted a human ruler, so God established a *monarchy*, with a king appointed by God.

4. Finally, the people were subjugated to other nations. Israel (and then the New Testament church) spent much of its time as a minority under foreign governments. These "subjugations" could probably be divided into two subcategories—*persecutorial*, where the ruling nation tried to restrict worship of the one true God, and *custodial*, where freedom to practice religion existed to some extent.

From studying biblical pluralisms, we learn not to be overly optimistic about the prospects for constructive interaction. In the biblical cases, conflict was twice as common as cooperation (92 conflicts and 46 cooperations). The instances of cooperation, however, leave substantial hope for good relationships—especially when one considers that the majority of conflicts (over 90 percent) took place in Old Testament political situations that are far different from twentieth-century America's situation.

Considering the differences between then and now, one might doubt that *any* lessons could be applied from the Bible to contemporary America.[10] Indeed, one might doubt whether there is much common ground *within* the Bible when one thinks of the differences between Old Testament wars and New Testament pronouncements on love and peace.

But on digging into the reasons behind the reasons for why God led his people to behave one way or another, we find much more consistency of principle than we might at first glance think possible. Three major streams of thought emerge. One is that we are commanded to love our neighbors unconditionally. The New Testament did not invent this expectation; in fact, it is an Old Testament command. Second, we are called to join with other believers to glorify God here on earth through institutions, whether an institution is the tribe, the temple, the monarchy, or the church. Third, we are to preach the truth of the gospel to any and all who will listen.

All three principles are required for a well-rounded theology of interfaith interaction. If any one principle is elevated as *the* principle of action, then relativism, triumphalism, or fanaticism will likely result. Our overall purpose through all three is to transform the world; each, however, brings a special piece to the puzzle of how transformation takes place. We will consider each one separately in the next three chapters.

Chapter 6

LOVING NEIGHBORS

I t is not difficult to like Maharagama Dhammasiri. A friendly,
middle-aged man from Sri Lanka, Dhammasiri has been in
this country for two years, and he loves America. Although he still
eats rice and curry, the staple diet of all Sinhalese, he also likes
American food—everything except fast food, that is.

Dhammasiri is also suspicious of fast conversation. He doesn't
talk glibly, but he answers questions with care, sometimes reflecting
for what seems like a few minutes before giving an answer. It is
obvious he would be a good counselor. His caring attitude comes
through even in the busiest times of his day.

What makes Maharagama Dhammasiri a bit unusual is the fact
that he is a Buddhist monk living in the heart of Washington, D.C.
He is the leader of the Washington Buddhist Vihara (temple) on 16th

Street in the Carter-Barron district of the city.

Within two or three blocks of his vihara, a veritable swarm of churches are situated. To the east are the Saint Paul AME Church on 14th Street and Saint Luke Baptist Church on Gallatin. Dhammasiri's immediate neighbors are Capitol Hill Interdenominational Temple and Christ Lutheran Church. A couple of blocks north is Sixth Presbyterian Church ("We celebrate our radically and culturally inclusive congregation") and a Spanish church, the Iglesia Evangelica Menonita. There is even another Buddhist church, the Chua Giac Hoang, a Buddhist Congregational Church of America that is made up largely of Southeast Asians.

Although Dhammasiri wears his bright yellow robes, people hardly bat an eye as he walks down the street in this particular district. The vihara itself is in an old three-story brick home. Across the street is a park. As I enter the vihara to talk to Dhammasiri, about fifteen kids are playing a game of soccer in the park; the three baseball diamonds stand empty.

Inside I find a bookstore on the enclosed porch, a large meditation room where the living/dining room used to be, and the kitchen. The second floor has Dhammasiri's office, his living quarters, and a library that is well stocked with books on Buddhism, original Pali texts, and about twenty Buddhist statues. A long table in the middle of the room is covered with stacks of envelopes, obviously from a mailing list, which I soon discover has two thousand names. About eight hundred members are active in the temple, 90 percent of whom are American citizens. The mailing is announcing the May celebration of Vesak, the Buddhist equivalent of both Christmas and Easter. This is the day on which the Buddha was born, was enlightened, and died. It is celebrated to honor the founder of the Buddhist tradition.

It is a bit odd to see the clash of cultures in this library. Along with the ancient Buddha statues and paintings are the modern accoutrements of a church: a stack of pressure-sensitive labels, a dictionary stand, an old, upright manual typewriter standing side-by-side with a newer IBM Selectric II. There is no computer, but there is a sign on the wall that reads, "Please do not smoke in the vihara."

We chat for a while about this vihara (the first Theravada temple built in the United States), some of its members, some of the reasons (meditation and peace) why Dhammasiri thinks Buddhism is attractive to Americans, and his hopes for the future of Buddhism in the United States.

I mention to Dhammasiri that I lived for a year in Sri Lanka. "When?" he asks. I tell him it was ten years ago. "How long since you've had a good plate of rice and curry?" I assure him it has been almost that long, since Americans can't really make rice and curry. "Come," he insists. After we go down to the kitchen, we sit and eat a plate of rice and curry together while we talk Sri Lankan politics.

It is not difficult to like Dhammasiri. He is a good neighbor—who happens to be a Buddhist living and working in America.

Love your neighbor
Of the three streams of thought that pervade the Bible's teaching about biblical pluralism, the one most obvious to the twentieth-century Christian is the command to love. Few of us have any difficulty with what we might call "Love Your Neighbor, Level One." This means sharing the common courtesies of life with the family that lives in the house next to ours, though that may occasionally be uncomfortable since the man of the house works at IBM and we work at Sperry-Rand, and the woman of the house thinks she should compete for Mrs. Illinois next year while we, at age 37, just put braces on our slightly protruding teeth. Furthermore, they have a pool and we don't. In spite of differences, we, because we are Christians, gather all our moral energy and speak pleasantly to our neighbors when called upon to do so, lend them our lawn mower when asked, watch their house when they are on vacation, and speak no ill of them even though we have occasion to do so. That is "Love Your Neighbor, Level One" in action.

The Bible, however, teaches "Love Your Neighbor, Level Two." Jesus, in particular, took the love-your-neighbor tradition of the Jewish Scriptures and preached it, embellished it, drew out some difficult implications of it, and then made it the law to end all laws, the one that summed up the entire teaching of the Jewish tradition. He made the breaking of what had once been a misdemeanor into a capital, treasonous offense. One of his followers, James, put an appropriate label on the phrase. He called love for neighbor the "Royal Law."

One of the most moving and instructive of all Jesus' stories in the New Testament is the one he told about one man helping another man—one whom he instinctively hated. The story grips us because it shows two of the most powerful instincts in the human psyche—self-preservation and species preservation—locked in mortal combat. It has a surprise ending when the normally weaker of the two instincts, concern for others, wins. It leaves us with a good feeling, the kind we used to have when our mother's bedtime stories ended on the expected right note, but it also leaves us with a sharp challenge when we are told to "go and do likewise."

The story is familiar:

> A man was going down from Jerusalem to Jericho, when he fell into the hands of robbers. They stripped him of his clothes, beat him and went away, leaving him half dead. A priest happened to be going down the same road, and when he saw the man, he passed by on the other side. So, too, a Levite, when he came to the place and saw him, passed by on the other side. But a Samaritan, as he traveled, came where the man was; and when he saw him, he took pity on him. He went to him and bandaged his wounds, pouring on oil and wine. Then he put the man on his own donkey, took him to an inn and took care of him. The next day he took out two silver coins and gave them to the innkeeper. "Look after him," he said, "and when I return, I will reimburse you for any extra expense you may have."

To make this story really hit home, a couple of substitutions help. First, identify yourself as one of the three men who had an opportunity to aid the injured man. Second, identify the injured man as one of a class of people you tend to dislike. Try, for example, black or white, Democrat or Republican, fundamentalist or secular humanist, rich or poor, abortionist or antiabortionist, foreigner (of many kinds), atheist, rapist, Communist, Hindu, Buddhist, or Muslim.

Only then does the story become real. Jesus teaches us that we must love such people. We must inconvenience ourselves in their favor, making their needs more important than our schedules. We must give them money when they need it. We must love them in all these ways though those we know and love best will probably not understand. We must love though we know that our friends would likely be more impressed if we adopted a kind of Rambo callousness and disregard for our enemies.

Jesus (and Paul, John, and others after them) often taught about love. Perhaps because Jesus was usually speaking to a Jewish audience, he made sure they knew that love was not a brand-new command but one with a long tradition in the Jewish Scriptures, the Old Testament. He always stretched his listeners in their understanding of what love really meant. And he would stress the supreme importance of love as a way of relating to other people.

The apostle Paul's teaching in the thirteenth chapter of Romans is a good example of these same elements.[1] In verse 8, Paul says that the person who loves his fellow man (*heteros*, a term that means any human being, not just a fellow Jew or Christian) has fulfilled the law—meaning, of course, the Jewish law. Paul then shows what he means by listing the more social of the Ten Commandments, the ones against murder, adultery, stealing, and coveting.

Some of the people listening to Paul would have thought of Old Testament commandments such as Leviticus 19:8 (which reads, "Love your neighbor as yourself") and verses in Exodus 23 that command us to take care of even an enemy's ox or donkey that we find wandering in our yard, or like another verse in the same chapter that says to treat aliens well. You yourselves were once aliens, the verse says, so treat aliens as you would want to be treated.

The core idea of loving enemies, which Jesus introduced in the fifth chapter of Matthew, was not new. Its context and application, however, were. No longer were "chosen people" being told to love the unchosen at little risk to themselves. They were being told to love people who had access to the same moral standing before God as they, the Jews, had. They were being told to love people who were perfectly capable of responding to love with hurtful behavior, because they were political equals or superiors to the Jews.

The parallel today, of course, is that we are asked to love Hindus, Buddhists, and Muslims, people who are no longer simply the object of foreign missionaries' concerns, or such tiny, insignificant groups that there is little risk to being nice. No, now we are asked to love people of growing power, people who pose a threat to the stability and traditions of our communities and churches. They may "take over the neighborhood." They may lead our children astray. They may badmouth us in the local newspaper. These people may use their emerging power to be nice *or* mean. They have the legal right to be either. It is a little harder to love under those circumstances. *That* is what was radical about the risky love Jesus was recommending.

Jesus, Paul, and others did not just teach this love as an afterthought—a law tacked on at the end of a longer list of the more important stuff. Look again at Romans 13: Paul said that love is the fulfillment of the law. "[W]hatever other commandment there may be [is] summed up in this one rule: Love your neighbor as yourself."

To be honest, it is this teaching that makes the freedom of religion tough to enjoy. Always before in America's history the problem of how to relate to other faiths was handled for us simply because there was basically only one socially acceptable religion. But now, everything is up for grabs. We like it that way, we want it that way, but—it puts the whole weight of responsibility for loving our neighbors right on our own shoulders.

Sometimes our shoulders sag with the strain. In March of 1987 George Gallup found that the groups that Americans least desired as neighbors were those of strange religious sects and cults. Forty-four percent of the people said they would not want to live next to someone who belonged to a cult. Second on the least-desired list of neighbors were religious fundamentalists—13 percent said they would not want one living next to them. (Blacks were tied at 13 percent.) Unmarried couples were fourth at 12 percent; Hispanics were fifth (9 percent), followed by Jews (3 percent), Protestants (2 percent), and Catholics (1 percent). When it comes to prejudice, religion seems to lead the race. (At least, people feel freer to admit to religious prejudice than racial prejudice.)[2]

Of course, intolerance is nothing new. Historically, strong feelings have often flared between Christians and non-Christians. On one occasion, according to Polycarp, a student of John the Disciple, the apostle was entering the baths at Ephesus. Inside he saw Cerinthus, a well-known gnostic, preparing to bathe. John, presumably garbed in a towel and a sour expression, rushed outside without taking a bath. "Let's flee," he said, "before the baths fall in. Cerinthus, the enemy of the truth, is inside." Obviously, this is an extreme example of someone avoiding a person of another faith. Or is it so extreme?[3]

Alongside religious intolerance is some evidence for a growing sense of tolerance. Another Gallup poll showed that those who say they would vote for a black, Jew, or Catholic for President have increased dramatically since the 1930s.[4] Most Americans (79 percent) favor the teaching of world religions in public schools.[5] A more recent survey by the Williamsburg Charter Foundation found that "there is a broad approval or acceptance of religion in public life." Only 13 percent felt there "is no place in America for the Muslim religion," and 60 percent approved of Buddhist chaplains in the armed forces. But other questions uncovered reservations about cults, Hare Krishna evangelism tactics, Satan worship, and TV preachers.

The word *tolerance* means different things to different people; I have already mentioned the need for a clearer definition. If tolerance means a basic acceptance (love) of one's neighbor, however, it is clearly a good thing, commanded by the strongest teachings in all of Scripture. And loving a neighbor must include developing a genuine understanding and interest in his religion. Hendrik Kraemer, the Dutch theologian and missiologist, noted the importance of establishing that kind of a relationship:

> The one point of contact between Christian and non-Christian religions is the disposition and the attitude of the missionary. The successful missionary must have an untiring and genuine interest in their religion, the ideas, the sentiments, the institutions—in short, in the whole range of life of the people among whom one works. Whosoever disobeys this rule does not find any real point of contact. Whosoever obeys it becomes one with his environment and has and finds contacts.[6]

Unfortunately, tolerance has come to be seen as an uncritical acceptance of ideas as well as people, and at that point it becomes not only an unscriptural teaching, but an intellectually dishonest one as well. We can love our neighbor as ourselves; we cannot believe our neighbor's ideas as we believe our own, the ones taught in Scripture.[7]

Jesus realized the command to love our neighbors was difficult.

Thus, he provided guidelines and aids to help us learn to obey it. Don't judge others, he said, or you will be judged in the same way. Our common sinful predicament should be a wonderful leveler in relationships with others.[8] Our understanding of God and the universe may be better than theirs, but this understanding does not necessarily make us morally better. We are not to judge.

Paul offered another guideline: In whatever way possible, we should remove barriers in our own personalities and culture in order to relate to others. We should try to be all things to all people without compromising our Christian witness.[9]

We should also realize that each neighbor is different and needs to be approached as a unique individual: "Be merciful to those who doubt; snatch others from the fire and save them; to others show mercy mixed with fear."[10] Lesslie Newbigin once said that "Christ doesn't make carbon copies, he makes originals."[11] We must avoid stereotypes and treat people as originals.

Two contexts of loving your neighbor

Jesus offered more than hints. Recognizing the difficulty of imperfect people trying to love other imperfect people, he suggested a context in which we can understand more clearly the meaning of loving one's neighbor. It is given in Matthew 22. There a Pharisee, a Jewish expert in the law, asks Jesus what the greatest commandment is. Jesus answers, " 'Love the Lord your God with all your heart, with all your soul, and with all your mind.' This is the first and greatest commandment. And the second is like it: 'Love your neighbor as yourself.' All the Law and the Prophets hang on these two commandments."

Love that does not grow out of love of God is not Christian love. It may look like it, act like it, and feel like it. But it is fundamentally flawed—like a home run being hit in the midst of a football game. It is a "good" thing, but it is not in the proper place.

This context may in some ways be seen as a limitation, a boundary to the command to love one's neighbor. Why do we need this boundary? First, because our love is always flawed, mixed with impure motives. If we were capable of perfect love, loving our neighbor would indeed be the only principle we needed. But we are not capable of perfect love. And wherever one sees a group establishing love as the *only* principle of Christian behavior, history has shown that heresy and apostasy will follow close behind.

Ethical principles must be measured against an absolute standard. The love standard of human beings, even the best human beings, is flawed. The only love standard we have is God. We must measure our love by the love of God.

The implications of this context are many, but perhaps the key one is that our love for neighbors will in the end be only as good as our love for God. If our relationship to God is poor, our relationship to Hindus, Buddhists, and Muslims will suffer. If our relationship to God is good, so will be our relationship to Hindus, Buddhists, and Muslims.

The finest example of this principle comes from the life of Jesus himself. He spent hours and hours helping other people, but he also spent time alone in what we might call strategic withdrawal from people.[12] He didn't sleep and read detective novels on those retreats. He prayed. Sometimes the most effective way to love your neighbor is to be alone and deepen your love for God.

There is a second context in which the command to love our neighbor must be understood. That context is the family. The family is used in Scripture as the Christian paradigm of love. God is our Father; we are his children. Christ loves the church as husbands are to love their wives. We are to obey God as a child is to obey his or her parents. Members of the church are brothers and sisters in Christ. We are to treat weaker Christians as we would act toward "weaker brothers"—with patient and persistent love.

What we learn from these biblical themes is a careful taxonomy of appropriate and inappropriate loving. Biblical loving is not a careless, carefree abandonment to emotional feeling. Love in a healthy family never is. Biblical loving is devotion of the *total* person, which means it has intellectual elements characterized by words such as *commitment* and *faithfulness*, and social elements characterized by words such as *responsibility* and *duty*. We *must* love—but we must do it with more than our hearts alone. We must do it with our minds and our spirits.

Early in the history of Christianity, some Egyptian Christians became fed up with the corruption and sinfulness of the church in the cities and towns. So they retreated to the desert and built monasteries where they tried to live out a purer form of the faith. One element of that faith was concern for non-Christians; the monks gave food to hungry bands of wandering Bedouins. In fact, the monks had a policy of never refusing someone who came to their gates and asked for help. Many Bedouins were grateful. Some, however, used the ruse of asking for food to get the monks to swing open the gates, whereupon they attacked and killed the monks and looted the monastery.

The monks were faced with a dilemma. Should they quit giving food? They felt that to deny it would be to disobey Christ's command to love their neighbors. Or should they give food and risk being killed? That would certainly erase their chance to be witnesses to the gospel.

They found a solution in what they called "Bedouin holes." All the monasteries standing in the Egyptian desert still have them: openings in the walls through which food could be lowered to hungry Bedouins without opening the gates and exposing the monks to dangerous Bedouin swords.

In the same way, our love for Hindus, Buddhists, and Muslims needs sometimes to be careful love. It is not that we are in danger of the sword! But, for example, how much do we expose our children to the world views of other faiths? At what ages would it be appropriate to take a child to a Nichiren Shoshu Buddhist service? (I have taken my child.) And at what age might it be inappropriate? (I only took one of my three children, the one I thought would understand.)

We want to guide our children to the point of making the Christian tradition their own, to insure the transmission of the faith to future generations. In some settings, in some situations, that may mean limiting contacts with other faiths. Paul appears to be speaking to such a situation in the Corinthian church.[13] But such situations should be seen as exceptional. The bias must always be toward engagement, interaction, and cooperation so that all the rich implications of loving one's neighbor can come through.

Love in balance
The biblical tradition of loving our neighbors is as strong as any. It is particularly strong in the passages dealing with biblical pluralisms. Jesus and the other New Testament writers elevated this teaching to

prime importance in the life of the Christian.

It is not the only teaching, however, that emerges from a study of biblical pluralisms. In order to be fully understood, it must be seen in concert with two others, one regarding the relationships of institutions representing Christian and non-Christian religions, and the other regarding the command to preach the truth.

To put it on a personal level: I am commanded to love Maharagama Dhammasiri, to sit and talk politics and eat rice and curry with him, to help him as a fellow human being. Even if he were not the likable person he is, that command would stand. But I am never to forget the institution he represents (and the Savior I represent). And at some point, my words or my life or both must witness to him of the Truth.

Chapter 7

THE CLASH OF
INSTITUTIONS

One element of dealing with Hindus, Buddhists, and Muslims can have a nasty, brutish reality about it. It is the clash of the institutions of these religious traditions (the mosques and temples) with the Christian institutions (the churches, denominations, and parachurch organizations). The clash at times involves the infighting of politics, the body blows of competition, and sometimes even the knockout punch of survival.

But the interaction is not always best described as a clash. Sometimes it means cooperation, friendly exchanges of speakers and worship services, and moral and material support for various projects each is working on—new buildings, camps for the kids, battles against drunk driving, or religiously threatening zoning laws before the city council. At times we find ourselves fighting on the same side. As cobelligerents we join forces in the common battle for moral decency.

This antiphonal dance between clash and cooperation can make the interaction between religious institutions seem ambiguous. It lacks the comforting clarity of the universal command to love your neighbors no matter what their religion or what cost to you. It lacks also the uncompromising sharpness of the command to preach the truth to a lost world. These two commands have an absolute quality about them. However difficult they may be to put into practice, they at least fit snugly in a comfortably logical box.

Institutional interaction is anything but snug. It is the *realpolitik* of religion. It rips the absolutes of our faith out from under their warm comforters and throws them out to do battle on the cold, concrete floor of the real world. When left alone, absolute commands to love our neighbor and preach the truth seem perfectly adequate, thank you. But put them in a real-life, real-world situation, and they don't always work out neatly.

Clash or cooperation? How is my church supposed to relate to that new Buddhist temple down the street? Should we ignore them? Warn against them? Visit them? Work with them on the interfaith drive to collect food for the hungry?

Several years ago a group of Chicago-area Hindu physicians met together and decided to build a temple in the western suburb of Aurora. They bought property on the edge of town (a cornfield, actually) and applied for a building permit. When area residents heard about the proposal, a campaign was started to ask the city council to deny the permit. Eventually, the permit was granted. The temple stands today, an almost-finished bit of India in the middle of Illinois.[1]

The interesting facet of the controversy, however, was the dilemma it posed for Christian churches: They were asked to choose sides. Many pastors found themselves wanting to choose both sides—or three sides. "We welcome them as neighbors," said one, reflecting a firm commitment to loving his neighbor. Said another, "I thank God for the religious freedom we have in this country. I realize that were we to deny that to this group we could be putting our own freedoms in danger," affirming the genius of this country's church-state policy. "Biblically oriented Christians in this community are naturally afraid of the propagation of the polytheistic faith in their community," said a third. The dilemma is that almost all pastors—and laypersons—agree with all three of those statements. It is the institutional church's responsibility to put them together and embody them in a consistent institutional policy. Mission impossible; good luck.

This very ambiguity in some sense makes our policy of the separation of church and state work. James Madison said as much in Federalist Paper Number 10: "A religious sect may degenerate into a political faction in a part of the Confederacy; but the variety of sects dispersed over the entire face of it must secure the national councils against any danger from that source."[2] Although Madison probably never dreamed his recipe for harmony would be used with such an extraordinary variety of religious traditions (he was thinking of balancing Christian denominations), from a purely political point of view it makes good sense.

It is unwise, however, to base one's ecclesiology on purely political considerations. It so happens that the biblical traditions teach nothing that conflicts with the principles of Madison's prescriptions. But the biblical teaching is based on far different assumptions and, indeed, goes far beyond them. To that teaching we now turn.

The biblical concern
The Bible's concern, in both Old and New Testaments, is to make sure that false teaching does not creep into the institutional church. The church must do the work of transforming society without itself being transformed. The church—with its theologians, denominations, pastors, and lay workers—is to avoid syncretism.

The Scriptures are full of such warnings: Paul's constant reminders to his fledgling congregations in Corinth, Galatia, Philippi; Jesus' warnings about false prophets; the Old Testament lessons of the Exile; the warnings against syncretism in the books of Kings and Judges; the lesson taught by the wandering Israelites' ill-fated golden calf; the stunning destruction of Sodom and Gomorrah. The institutions of God's people—whatever form they take in Scripture—are to keep themselves pure.[3]

The concern about purity is natural. A religious institution is a group of people banded together for the purpose of carrying on a tradition, of mutually experiencing that tradition, and of modeling that tradition to a watching world. All of these purposes demand a fidelity to the essence of the teaching—ergo, the almost paranoid concern with purity and continuity, not only in Christian tradition, but in nearly every religious community.

This quest for purity does not entirely explain, however, the extraordinary diversity we find in the Bible. Sometimes interaction with other competing institutions is violent and hostile. Sometimes it is friendly. Sometimes, in keeping with the fallen nature of the world, it is ambiguous.

Some would explain these differences in terms of whether God's people are being faithful or unfaithful to God's commands. But that explanation does not hold consistently. Sometimes God commanded total destruction of a rival institution, sometimes cooperation. (These commands were followed by varying degrees of obedience).

Two variables are worth noting briefly here and in more detail later. First, in the Old Testament the theological, social, and political aspects of God's people were all under the same institutions. In these circumstances, confrontations with peoples of other world views were more sharp-edged. Religious purity and political existence were synonymous, thus "holy wars" were logical. This situation changed, of course, when the New Testament gospel crossed freely over political and social barriers.[4]

Second, God's people treated other religious institutions positively or negatively depending on their attitude toward God and Jesus Christ. Respect seemed to breed respect (or at least neutrality), and disrespect bred hostility. This attitude is most prominent in Old Testament teachings. But even Jesus warned against giving to "dogs what is sacred." He said, "Do not throw your pearls to pigs. If you do, they may trample them under their feet, and then turn and tear you to pieces."[5]

Three approaches to interchurch/temple/mosque relations appear in Scripture: cooperative competition, neutral competition, and hostile competition. It is worth looking at each of these in turn.

Cooperative competition

The Old Testament examples of this type of cooperation are many. Abraham, for one, carried on extensive negotiations with other

Semitic clans and with the powerful Egyptian dynasty. He was often foolish in how he behaved toward other groups, but his intent was obviously to coexist peacefully—and get food in times of famine.[6]

Another example: Jeremiah predicted and Ezra related and carried out the rebuilding of the temple at Jerusalem with the endorsement of the decidedly un-Christian king of Persia, Cyrus. The Lord moved the heart of Cyrus to help the Israelite captives return to their homeland and reconstruct their temple. From Cyrus's point of view, this ploy was part of a political strategy to control subject peoples by allowing them to worship their gods freely. He treated the Babylonians and their religious institutions the same.[7]

Perhaps the most interesting of all the cooperative arrangements in the Old Testament, however, was between Hiram, the king of Tyre, and his contemporaries David and Solomon.[8] Hiram ruled for thirty-five years over Phoenicia, a successful sea-trading empire north of Israel, part of present-day Lebanon. Under Hiram's rule, Tyre became the leading city of Phoenicia and the center of a trading empire that touched all parts of the Mediterranean.

Hiram became David's ally against the Philistines. In controlling them together, David and Hiram in effect became trading confederates, with David protecting the inland trading routes, Hiram the sea lanes. When David needed raw materials to build his palace at the newly conquered fortress of Jerusalem, Hiram supplied him not only with cedar logs, but with artisans and stonemasons as well. In return, David probably sent food. David made a treaty with Hiram and had peaceful relations with the pagan king all his life.

The peaceful relations were continued under Solomon's reign. When Solomon inherited his father's throne, he began to build the temple his father had planned. Hiram supplied cedar and pine logs; in exchange, Solomon sent Hiram wheat and olives. (Tyre had long been dependent on Israel for agricultural products.) Like his father before him, Solomon maintained peaceful relations with Hiram.

Several considerations about Hiram's relationship with David and Solomon are noteworthy. First, Hiram initiated the relationship, probably when he saw David would be the dominant player in Canaanite politics. It was a smart but sincere gesture of good will. The two kingdoms needed each another.

Second, the relationship went beyond isolated trade. It involved teams of Israelite workers laboring with Sidoneon artisans and vice versa. When Solomon asked that the cedars of Lebanon be cut for the temple, he specified, "[M]y men will work with yours" on the logging project. Earlier, Hiram had sent artisans to Jerusalem to work with David's men in building the palace. Apparently this interethnic work force was effective.

Third, Hiram displayed great respect for the God of Israel. At one point in the negotiations with Solomon, Hiram noted in admiration, "Praise be to the Lord," a reference to the power and glory of Yahweh. Whether this was simply good politics or sincere respect for Israel's God (or both) from this pagan king, it is hard to say. But it must have aided their friendly relations.

It probably helped smooth over some of the rough spots in the relationship, too. It appears the balance of trade got somewhat out of kilter (in Hiram's favor), and Solomon had to put up twenty towns in Galilee as collateral. Hiram was not impressed with their quality and called them the Land of Cabul. But he bided his time and eventually Solomon rebalanced the trade deficit with gold.

The Hiram/David/Solomon association is a good example of friendly relationships between two groups in spite of deep ideological differences. Obviously, though, not all relationships are quite so positive.

Neutral cooperation
At times, relationships between those with other world views can be described as neither hostile nor friendly. One thinks of the Gibeon-ites who originally tricked Joshua into a treaty of neutrality by pretending to be from a long way off, when in reality they lived just over the next hill. Because he had given his word, Joshua felt constrained to honor the treaty, although the Gibeonites were reduced to the status of woodcutters and water carriers. David later also honored this treaty.[9]

This relationship could not be called friendly. It had elements of deceit and trickery about it that prevented it from becoming a warm relationship like that between Hiram and Israel. Nor might it be called a totally hostile arrangement. The Gibeonites reached an understanding, which Joshua honored. Later Saul violated it by killing some of the Gibeonites, but David re-established the understanding and made amends for Saul's excesses. The relationship can best be described as neutral cooperation.

Neutral cooperation describes several other biblical relationships. Joseph working in Egypt might be one example.[10] So might the agreement reached by the wandering Israelites with the Edomites to pass through their land without fighting.[11] On some occasions, tribute was paid to maintain a balance of power. King Joash paid Hazael, a king of Aram, to keep him from attacking Jerusalem.[12] This payment was not a friendly accommodation, but it was an accommodation all the same. Sometimes tribute went the other way.

Several consequences about neutral competition are worthy of notice. First, a real, mutually beneficial exchange of goods and services results. These associations are not for the sake of association, but they are business deals. Joseph was a skilled administrator in Egypt. He did his job better than anyone else. Joash bought safety for Jerusalem with his tribute—he wasn't buying real friendship. Likewise, the Edomites never became good friends with Israel—they simply decided they would rather allow safe passage to the Israelite army than fight them.

Second, the agreements never involved a compromise of religious values. At least, compromise was never part of the official package, although it sometimes happened.

Third, attitudes seem to differentiate this class of relationships from hostile relationships. Conflict is not always absent. But the conflict is usually the result of mistaken perceptions rather than malice or ill will. A good example is the story of Simon in Acts 8. Simon was a sorcerer, an occupation vigorously condemned in all of Scripture.[13] He carried on his business in Samaria, and both the people of Samaria and he himself viewed his powers as great. The Samaritans, however, heard the gospel, believed it, and were ministered to by Peter and John. When Simon saw the powerful effect of the Holy Spirit on his clientele, he tried to buy the "magic" from Peter and John. They rebuked him. Rebuffed, Simon backed off and even asked the apostles to pray for him so he would not suffer for his mistake.

Perhaps he was converted. Other statements in the passage, however, cast doubt upon his possible conversion. It appears that

Simon simply recognized the power of God, knew it was real, and asked for an accommodation to protect himself.

Hostile competition

A third class of interactions can only be called hostile. The most outstanding examples are those involving the Israelites as they fought to occupy the promised land of Canaan.[14] Joshua was told to destroy every living person and animal in the city of Jericho—except Rahab and her family. Likewise, Saul was told to kill every living thing associated with the Amalekites—men, women, children, infants, and even livestock. David killed thousands of his enemies, particularly Philistines. These brutal massacres have bothered Christians for two thousand years, and several points must be made about their context before we can draw general principles from them.

First, these massacres took place in a setting where religion and politics were one and the same. Because God had selected Israel as his special carrier of truth, political survival was inextricably intertwined with religious purity. There was no separation of church and state. Separation became religiously possible only after the universalized ethical teachings of Isaiah and other prophets culminated in the coming of Jesus the Messiah. Jesus did away with the old situations and proclaimed the gospel for everyone: Jew, Greek, barbarian. In practical terms, Jesus' coming meant that never again would a political system or a physical place on earth have quite as much importance as it did in Old Testament times.

Second, the motive for the Old Testament massacres was institutional purity, not xenophobia. The morals of the pagans were questionable, to be sure; but the morals of the Israelites, especially in their darker moments, were no bargain either. God was constantly warning them to shape up. Thus, the motive for conquering the land with such a scorched-earth policy was to carve out a physical place where the *structures* of institutional purity could be constructed. Any threat to that purity from either without or within the community had to be dealt with in the harshest of terms.

Third, the commands of God don't always fit our human understanding of pure justice. We see the short range, we understand imperfectly, we act inconsistently. God doesn't. God's people must obey even when they don't completely understand the mystery of God's purposes.

When seen in the light of these conditions, the principles we can draw from Old Testament hostile competition seem to be consistent with those of cooperative and neutral competition: The primary consideration in interinstitutional interaction is purity. Cooperation is not ruled out, but if the other party threatens the purity of the church, he must be rebuffed with whatever means are needed.

Consider two New Testament examples:

When Jesus visited the temple in Jerusalem, he discovered financial corruption on the holy ground itself. He physically attacked the perpetrators, denouncing them in the strongest language.[15] Impurity is now seen in the context of the religious institution (the temple), not the state and its political structure.

When faced with the quasi-political structure (the Sanhedrin and most certainly with the Romans in Matthew 26 and 27), Jesus was silent, perhaps partly out of his recognition of God's plan in these events, but also because the battlefield of engagement had shifted from the purity of his "Father's house" to the purity of the state. The New Testament reaction to hostile world views is no less vigorous than the Old Testament's, but the means used and the scene of battle had shifted noticeably.

What are the implications for today? There are no holy nations (America included) or holy grounds (Israel and the Vatican included) to crusade for, but the purity of the bride of Christ, the church, must be energetically defended.

Let's be clear: Our very strong preference should be for peaceful relations. For one thing, our ideal of loving our neighbors should mitigate a hostile posture wherever possible.

There is also a pragmatic reason. Friendly cooperation is more *effective*. By joining forces on moral issues we have a better chance of implementing crucial moral reforms our secularized nation desperately needs. More important, if our ultimate aim is to transform the world, we have a better chance of doing so in an atmosphere of cooperative competition than hostile competition.

Ask yourself this question: What kind of people switch from one hostile army to another? The answer is traitors, the weakest people in the other camp. The intelligent will only dig in their heels and stay the course if relations between the two groups are radicalized. Friendly cooperation leaves the door open for people to see the truth of Jesus Christ's message.

Furthermore, few non-Christians just "drop in" to our churches anymore. If we want to preach to more than just "the Christian choir," we need to go out and put ourselves in places to do it. Cooperative ventures offer at least a lifestyle witness.

How to categorize

For teaching purposes I have tried to draw three distinct pictures of possible ways of relating to temples and mosques. In reality, they are on a continuum. At one end is close, cordial cooperation. At the other is separation, or perhaps under some conditions, hostile engagement.

Are there guidelines that will help us in knowing how to respond? Four questions can be asked:

1. *Is the theological integrity of the church threatened?* The answer to this question may not only determine the level and style of interaction, but which members of the church should be involved. In some cases, should only the most mature believers be assigned to represent the body?

2. *What is the other group's attitude toward God/Christ?* We have already noted Hiram's show of respect for the Lord, and suggested it as one reason David and Solomon developed such a good, long-lasting relationship with him. We should also note the easy, open entry given the wise men from the East who came to see the baby Jesus. Why? Because they had seen his star in the East and wanted to worship him.

Hindus, Buddhists, and Muslims who worship in institutions that claim at least basic respect for Jesus Christ should be considered candidates for cobelligerent causes. Those who do not, need to be handled circumspectly, if at all.[16]

3. *Will association result in actions that display the fruit of the Spirit?* Whatever we do, and with whomever we do it, we want our witness to include love, joy, peace, patience, kindness, goodness, faithfulness, gentleness, and self-control. The degree to which that can be accomplished in interfaith relations should be a factor in deciding what those relations should be.[17]

The basic moral codes of Hinduism, Buddhism, and Islam are admirable. Committed adherents of these religious traditions are often moral people. Their morality does not make them Christians, but it does signal that the institutions they represent may be good candidates for friendly competition.

4. *Are we aware of the Holy Spirit's presence in this relationship?* Perhaps a paradigm for this principle can be found in Jesus' parting comments to his disciples before his ascension. He reminded them that they were to be witnesses to the gospel—that Christ suffered, died, and rose so that repentance, forgiveness, and holiness could be preached, taught, and developed in Jews and Gentiles everywhere. But then Jesus warned his disciples to stay in the city until the power of the Holy Spirit came upon them.[18]

Interaction with adherents of other religious traditions has an element of risk about it. Yet we are commanded to take such risks. In order to protect ourselves and the integrity of the gospel tradition, we must be sure our motives are not selfish, prideful, or unknown. For that reason we need to know that the Holy Spirit is in whatever we do.

Other less institutional questions arise as well:

● Can we combine the biblical command to love our neighbors with the equally strong command to make our churches strong transformers of the non-Christian world?

● Can we get along with people and still disagree with them?

● Can we like and admire people of other faiths and yet not doubt our basic faith convictions?

● Can we be nice to people though we think they are wrong?

To answer these questions, we need to look at what the Bible says about preaching the truth.

Chapter 8

PROCLAIMING THE TRUTH

The world has always been a battlefield of warring ideas. The serpent suggested a different way of living to Eve, and he was persuasive enough to convince her to try it. Ever since, the ebb and flow of history has been matched by the point and counterpoint of ideas: Plato's ideal versus Aristotle's mean between the extremes; Eastern monism versus Western dualism; Christian orthodoxy versus heretical ideas about the nature of Christ; socialism versus capitalism. The list of ideas fought for and against is endless.

Our age is no different. Abortionists and antiabortionists wage ideological war in state legislatures and in front of abortion clinics. Pornographers print and publish even as antipornographers lobby for laws to stop them. The Moral Majority, which claimed to represent grassroots America, argued the benefits of the Judeo-

Christian ethic. The People for the American Way, claiming the warrant of a 200-year-old American civil religion, endorsed what the breathless announcer for the television series "Superman" used to call "truth, justice, and the American way."

The world is not a place for the faint of heart—or mind. Unfortunately, the faint of mind have gained sway in modern American life. Apparently cowed by the prospect of unending ideological battle, these people have successfully sold the idea that we need not argue quite so passionately for our positions. The reason, they believe, is that all ideas have relatively equal truth value. Everything would be just fine if we would simply accommodate one another in a sort of "think and let think" atmosphere of mutual respect.

Many have shown the logical fallacies that make this relativism an unusually weak philosophy to live by. "History and the study of cultures do not teach or prove that values and cultures are relative."[1] Yet the most damning argument is that relativism has itself become an absolute principle used *intolerantly* against anyone who dares to proclaim absolute principles.

When it comes to confronting the world religions, relativism proves itself not only logically futile, but ineffective as well. It simply doesn't work. People do not view their religious beliefs as culturally conditioned options: They *believe* them.

What is religious belief? Religions attempt to answer the ultimate questions of life, and that is what makes religion different from economic or philosophic theories, which change almost as rapidly as the Dow Jones Index. As William Wilberforce wrote, "Religion is religion because it demands, like nothing else, a final answer."[2] Religion answers ultimate questions with divinely given principles. You can change religions, of course, but while you hold one you must believe it is absolute or else you don't really have "faith."

Jesus said that his way is the only way, that no one can truly live in God without recognizing the absolute truth of his teaching. "I am the way, the truth, and the life," he said. "No man comes to the Father but by me."[3]

The Bible is clear that we must engage in the never-ending battle of ideas. Jesus himself set the pattern when, as a twelve-year-old boy, he wandered away from his parents in Jerusalem's jammed holiday streets and ended up in the Jewish temple debating the fine points of religion. Later in his life he always made time for such debates—sometimes with religious professionals, sometimes with down-and-outers such as prostitutes, divorced women, crooked government officials, and thieves. The clash of ideas beat out the rhythm of Jesus' life and ministry.[4]

One way or the only way?
Today we proclaim the truth of Jesus as Lord in a climate of religious pluralism. American religious scholars offer three ways of responding to this climate. One is to accept pluralism not only as a fact, but as the way life should be. This attitude of *normative* pluralism claims that all religions are culturally conditioned attempts by men to respond to one ultimate reality. Jesus Christ and Christianity are no more unique than the Buddha and Nirvana. They are simply different ways of looking at the same thing.[5] This position is very similar to the one held by many Hindus.

A second, specifically Christian, way of responding claims a uniqueness and necessity for what Jesus Christ did on the cross, but denies that knowing about Jesus and his work is necessary for salvation. Thus, good Buddhists or Hindus will probably go to heaven even though they may never know or accept that they do so because of the work of Jesus. This position is called *inclusivism.*[6]

A third way of responding is called *exclusivism.* This position holds both that the work of Jesus Christ is unique and that a hard-and-fast condition of salvation is that one accepts him and his work by name. Put more simply, for the exclusivist, Christianity is the right religion and all other religions are wrong.[7]

In our current cultural climate, the concept that one idea is right and others wrong is unfashionable. Those who hold exclusivist religious positions are often viewed as intellectual troglodytes. Yet orthodox Christians have always been exclusivists; Jesus himself was an exclusivist. We need to show that our commitment to absolute standards is a good thing. Without developing this point in depth, I would suggest the following:

1. *The inescapability of exclusivism.* Everyone has absolutes and lives by them. Even the current climate of relativism is a commitment to one absolute value—relativism.

2. *The honesty of exclusivism.* Conscious commitment makes for

honest living. It allows better discussions; two people who are clear about their commitments can better identify their differences—and similarities.

3. *The value of exclusivism.* People who accomplish great things are almost always committed. Few will give their lives for a cause that is relatively true.

Changing ground

We have an obligation to proclaim the truth in the battlefield of ideas, as Christians always have and always will. But our modern situation makes this more difficult. Relativism is more than a philosophy; it has become a way of life.

Consider, for example, the impact of the news media. On a recent morning I spent a couple of hours reading the Sunday *New York Times.* On a pad of lined yellow paper, I noted any articles that dealt with religion in general—Hinduism, Buddhism, and particularly Islam. My list included stories on Salman Rushdie's anti-Muslim novel, *The Satanic Verses,* sectarian religious murders in Northern Ireland, American archbishops meeting with the Pope in Rome, Buddhist priests rioting in Tibet, a play about angels being staged in Italy, Muslims winning thirty local elections in Israel, the ethics of Sen. John Tower, rights abuses in Venezuela, a neo-Nazi revival in West Germany, and the progress of civil rights in the United States.

That same afternoon I spent a couple of hours in front of the microfiche machine at the public library, reading the Sunday *New York Times* of twenty years earlier. Again looking for articles dealing with religion, I noted stories on German evangelicals, Czech officials honoring Auschwitz's Jews, Jewish scholarship, and liberal British Catholics.

Obviously, something has changed. Religion has become a topic that the *Times* has decided deserves increased coverage. But religions other than Christianity are also being covered because world events have forced the press to focus more on other religions. The Middle East political situation cannot be understood without a good grasp of Islam. Sinhalese-Tamil clashes in Sri Lanka cannot be fully fathomed without knowing the Buddhist-Hindu components of the struggle.

More and more Americans, whether they like it or not, are becoming used to suppositions previously foreign to Western Christian thinking. Stories in the news media about religion flood us with beliefs as varied (and apparently morally neutral) as one's choice of cuisine.

The middle of the world

Another force shaping our cultural climate is world commerce. I live in a middle-class town of 50 thousand located halfway between the urban center of downtown Chicago and the rural farms of Illinois's corn country. If I can find traces of the Middle and Far East here, chances are I can find them almost anywhere in the United States.

I can buy the *New York Times* at the Wheaton Pharmacy on Hale Street. Three blocks east, I enter the Jewel supermarket. There, amid hamburger, chicken, corn, and apple pie, I find the typical Chinese and Japanese foods—bean sprouts, chow mein, Suzi Wan dinners, LaChoy frozen dinners, and Kikkoman soy sauce. I also find sushi, tofu, bok choy, cous cous, ginger root, and cherimoya.

Two blocks north I pass a Vietnamese restaurant, the Nha Hang, and I take a left to enter Toad Hall, the local bookstore. Toad Hall has many books on oriental art, Eastern religions, and "kung fu" westerns. (*Books in Print* tells us that 285 books are currently available under the subject heading "Hinduism," 758 under "Buddhism," and 675 under "Islam." Scores of publishers with names such as Shambhala, Advaita Ashrama, and the Islamic Center publish nothing but books on these subjects.)

Two blocks south is another bookstore that sells comic books. My three sons, David, Paul, and Joseph, read *Mad, Cracked,* and *Sports Illustrated for Kids* respectively, but as I scan the titles offered, I realize they could have chosen comics with titles like *Ninjas and Superspies, Buddha's Palm, Oriental Heroes, Cosmic Odyssey, Kiku San,* or *Teenage Mutant Ninja Turtles* (my favorite!).

Almost every major shopping center has outlets of major Eastern import chains, such as Asian House, Oriental Interiors, Pier One Imports, Double Happiness Corporation, and Jade by Chang. I would guess that thousands of houses in my town have at least some rooms decorated with Oriental motifs.

By itself, none of these influences would change our way of thinking, of course. But cumulatively, they do shift the paradigms that order our thoughts. Some do it more directly than others.

Perhaps the most popular new films of recent years were those in George Lucas's *Star Wars* trilogy. The action is patterned after American Old West, high-noon shoot-outs, but the thought forms behind the characters' motivations are based on pure Eastern monism.

This philosophy is evident throughout the films, but one scene is particularly telling. In it, Luke Skywalker, the hero, is on his way to save the good guys from the universe's bad guys, but he is young and untrained. His mentor is Obi-wan Kenobi, an older master who uses a spiritual power called "The Force" to overcome evil. The third character in the following dialogue is Han Solo, the "secular human-ist" of the bunch. The scene involves Luke practicing with his light saber, a laser sword, against a remote-controlled enemy:

Kenobi: Remember, a Jedi can feel "The Force" flowing through him.

Luke: You mean it controls your actions?

Kenobi: Partially. But it also obeys your commands.

Solo: Hokey religions and ancient weapons are no match for a good blaster at your side, kid.

Luke: You don't believe in the Force, do you?

Solo: Kid, I've flown from one side of this galaxy to another. I've seen a lot of strange stuff, but I've never seen anything to make me believe there's one all-powerful force controlling everything. There's no mystical energy field that controls my destiny. It's all a lot of simple tricks and nonsense. *(The remote-control "enemy" is easily getting the best of Luke.)*

Kenobi: I'd suggest you try it again, Luke. This time let go of your conscious self and act on instinct. *(Kenobi puts a helmet on Luke that blindfolds him.)*

Luke: But with the blast shield down, I can't even see. How am I supposed to fight?

Kenobi: Your eyes can deceive you. Don't trust them. *(The enemy still beats him. Luke redoubles his concentration.)*

Stretch out your feelings. *(Luke succeeds in defeating his enemy.)* You see? You can do it.

Luke: You know, I did feel something. I could almost feel the remote.

Kenobi: That's good. You've taken your first step to a larger world.[8]

The lack of ordered ideas

What does all this mean? It means there are a lot of incompatible ideas floating around. Polls show that 85 percent of the American people believe that Jesus Christ is the divine Son of God. Those same polls also show that 23 percent believe in reincarnation.[9] Most view creation as an act of a personal God who made the world from nothing. But few would quarrel with such statements as "God is really within us" and "Discovering God is the same as discovering ourselves." These ideas are sometimes packaged in clearly Eastern clothing, but sometimes they are just floating around in music and films without any identification whatsoever.

The problem is not just that these incompatible ideas are floating around in America's intellectual ether. There have always been ideas that challenge Christians in our culture, and there always will be. Indeed, challenging ideas rarely lead to the enervation of Christianity; they usually strengthen it. "Iron sharpens iron," Proverbs says, and this wisdom has shown true over and over.

Further, the presence of these ideas need not signal sinister designs by the people who promulgate them. As a matter of fact, most Eastern influences are morally neutral. The presence of Oriental motifs in interior decorating cannot be traced to a malevolent source. Eastern influences are present because of increased immigration from Asia, the globalization of trading markets, the shrinking size of the world, and the curiosity of the American mind, always searching for better, and more beautiful, ways of doing and thinking about things. Few Oriental influences can be traced to any kind of religious thought at all. Thus you have the mayor of New York City saying that "graffiti on the walls of trains or subway stations creates bad karma," and Hollywood actress Uma Thurman choosing the name of a Hindu diety for her stage name.[10] We need not see an evil conspiracy behind their choice of words or names.

The problem lies with the apparent inability of Americans to discriminate between ideas, to identify them for what they are, and to put them together in meaningful patterns. The idea of developing a coherent philosophy of life, once fundamental to being an educated person, is especially foreign to younger Americans. They have not been trained to see how ideas and behaviors cohere. "If it feels good, do it" has replaced "Just use good, common sense" as the byword of popular ethics. No longer are there consistent, identifiable roots upon which to base one's common sense. Students are trained to use therapeutic techniques to get in touch with their feelings instead of being shown how to discern the good, the true, the rationally consistent.

Ideas on the fast track

Consider also the speed with which new thought forms arise, capture the public imagination, undergo evaluation, and either become part of the national culture or die. It used to be that this process took years. The slow pace provided something of a safety net because it gave the slowest actors in the process, the philosophers and cultural observers, time to reflect and locate these new ideas and trends in a larger overall pattern, and then to spot warning signals. The speed with which these trends now come and are marketed nationwide has put a serious crimp in the philosopher's (and theologian's) style. Leisurely reflection is not quick enough to keep some of the more dangerous ideas from taking root.

The public still demands evaluation, but at a speed that leaves most true scholars and thinkers dazed. Presenting a paper at a professional conference two years down the road is not quick enough—we need the wisdom now. And into this breach has stepped our culture's intellectual version of the fast-food restaurant, the journalists. These writers blithely comment on every passing trend with a quick thumbs-up or thumbs-down. If necessary, they can bring in agreeable scholars (and even a token "dissenter") for a quick quote, but the journalists control the overall picture. Since we are moving too fast to wait for a more reflective judgment, the journalists' responses are marketed to every nook and cranny of the culture, and judgment that used to take years is passed within a matter of days, sometimes even hours.

This speed makes it virtually impossible to formulate coherent systems of thought, especially since the whole idea of systematic thinking is out of style. The absence of a coherent and systematic, critical mechanism leads to the final point of the problem: *The actual embrace of this free-floating hodgepodge of ideas is a good thing.* Systems restrict and confine—so the thinking goes. It is far better just to let everyone do his or her own thing; damn the consistency, full speed ahead. This attitude is relativism as a lifestyle.

The best example of this whole process is the New Age movement.[11] Never really a movement, it typifies the modern marketing approach to ideas and their implications. The New Age is a bewildering melange of Eastern and self-help ideas with no internal consistency at all. These ideas include beliefs in channeling, crystals, reincarnation, UFOs, gnostic ways of knowing, pyramids, and hundreds of other weirdnesses. They are held together primarily by two suppositions: that everything is God, and that the best way to know God is to know oneself (since everyone is part of God). New Age advocates do not preach doctrine; they provide services to aid you in your search. They do not attempt to figure out what is true; they provide options for you to chose from—the more the better. This consumer mentality toward ideas makes the presence of world religions in our midst particularly problematic. We simply do not have today the tools (or the resolve and training to use the tools) to discriminate between the true and the false.

The solution is not to go on an iconoclastic ax-swinging tour, destroying every trace of Eastern and Middle Eastern influence. The solution is to locate those ideas that underlie Hindu and Buddhist thought. In those contexts, they can be evaluated and mined for insights in evangelism and apologetics. This discernment is an essential aspect of proclaiming the gospel in the face of other religions. We do not merely offer Christianity as one more religious service on a menu of possibilities. We attempt to show its unique truthfulness in the face of other religions' truth claims.

When clearly explained and understood, Hindu, Buddhist, and Muslim ideas are not dangerous to us. Neither are Hindu and Buddhist temples nor Islamic mosques. Least dangerous of all are our Asian and Middle Eastern neighbors. Rather, they are opportunities for us to love our neighbors, and in so doing, to proclaim the truth.

Chapter 9

PRINCIPLES OF PROCLAIMING THE TRUTH

The clash of religious ideas, of course, can be dangerous. The argument is not about inconsequential matters—like choosing what to have for supper. It is about serious questions. The ultimate issues of life, death, and meaning ride on the outcome.

For exclusivists, such conversation is not just for personal intellectual satisfaction. The goal is transformation, attempting to metamorphize the world through these ideas. Exclusivists want to convince, persuade, and restructure in order to make truth and justice more visible in a false and unjust world.

Anyone undertaking such an ambitious and dangerous task is wise to sketch some guidelines in advance. Because the Bible is full of world-view clashes, it offers a rich store of principles for use in both formal and informal interchanges with non-Christian world views.

1. Master your own faith.

You cannot fully articulate your faith to others until you can articulate it to yourself. A conversation with a person of another tradition becomes meaningless blather if you enter it not knowing where you stand on key issues. Sharing mutual uncertainties may have some therapeutic value, but it certainly does not make for intelligent conversation.

Understanding your own faith does not mean that a full systematic expertise is required; it does mean that a firm commitment to the implications of a simple John 3:16 gospel is. Richard Baxter, in *The Reformed Pastor*, had some good advice: "Do not make a creed any longer than God has made."[1]

Neither does it require an arrogant, I-can-be-taught-nothing attitude. On the contrary, an attitude of confident openness is consistent with a commitment to truth, an assurance of faith, and a genuine love for all, Christian and non-Christian.

2. Be prepared for conflict.

Jesus didn't mince any words about what his teaching would do to people: "Do you think I came to bring peace on earth? No, I tell you, but division. From now on there will be five in one family divided against each other, three against two and two against three. They will be divided, father against son and son against father, mother against daughter and daughter against mother, mother-in-law against daughter-in-law and daughter-in-law against mother-in-law."[2]

The gospel is a message that precludes neutrality. Once you hear it, you must decide to be for or against it. After choosing, you will be on the other side of the fence from those who choose differently. They will argue with you. In some cases, they will bring pressure to bear for change.

Fortunately, several factors help mitigate this pressure:
- the peace of God in our hearts;
- our commitment to love all our neighbors;
- the laws of our country allowing freedom to worship for all religions;
- the knowledge that Jesus, too, was attacked by those who disliked his teaching.[3]

3. Recognize truth in other religions.

One-sided conversations are not really conversations. People respond to ideas much more readily if they are convinced they have something to offer in the interchange. The Bible tells us that adherents of other faiths hold two experiences, or potential experiences, in common with Christians.

First, there is an awareness of God. Paul makes it clear in his letter to the Roman Christians that God has made himself known to all men and women. Illumination comes mainly through the beauty, order, and mystery of the created world.

Second, all humans have an innate sense that something is wrong, that they do not quite measure up to some standard. Men and women do not always know what is wrong or what the standard is—but they do recognize a need for something beyond themselves.

These two facts of human existence mean that we can have genuine two-way conversations with those of other faiths. We can listen to them. We can learn from them. And in our openness, they can learn from us.[4]

The key is to start where your dialogue partner is, as Paul did in his famous sermon to the Athenians in Acts 17. The unknown god represented the principle of natural revelation that Paul articulated so well in Romans 1. In Acts 17, we see him using a theological insight in a homiletical setting. The same principle can apply to one-on-one or small-group conversations.

In these more intimate settings, sociological and cultural realities take on increased significance. If we know, for example, that the segregation of the sexes is extremely important for Middle Eastern immigrants, allowance can be made for their sensitivities. Cross-cultural communication is an art. Learning to separate these important realities from the essence of the gospel can greatly aid discussion.

4. Accept the irony of the situation.

Religious conversations exhibit a certain incongruence, which always seems a little like grown men playing with toy guns or small boys and girls dressing up in their daddy's or mommy's clothes. There is good reason for this charade. It looks something like the following:

- As Christians, we are arguing for an absolute standard of truth;
- Yet our understanding of that truth, because of sin and ignorance, is only partial;
- Our conversation partner also believes in absolute truth (whether consciously or unconsciously);
- Yet he or she has only partial understanding.

The potential for miscommunication is great. For example, one of us (or both) can use our commitment to absolute truth like a hammer to smash the other's partial, imperfect understanding. Conversation becomes indoctrination or worse.

The best conversations occur between two partners who fully understand the truth of all four of the above statements. Any conversation that falls short of that understanding degenerates into mutual monologues or dishonest accommodation.

5. Consider your motives.
T. S. Eliot put it best when he said, "This then is the final treason; to do the right thing for the wrong reason."[5] The Bible is full of similar warnings against behavior that traces the letter of the law perfectly, but is done with fastidiousness and arrogance that destroys the spirit. There are many dangerous motives we can bring to the clash of world views:

Scalp hunting—forgetting that we are but one link in the long chain of transformation. Paul planted, Apollos watered, but God gave the growth.[6]

Manipulation—mistaking high-pressure salesmanship for the simple, honest telling of the gospel.

Arrogance—forgetting that we, too, are sinners and that "there but for the grace of God, go [we]."

6. Set limited goals for the discussion.
Discussions accomplish only so much. Several factors make this statement true. First, salvation is by faith alone. We can present fine syllogisms, but unless faith is stirred, conversion does not take place. Second, as we have already noted, our role may only be seed planting; someone else may be called to do the watering. Sure conversion comes only by the Holy Spirit.

Lesslie Newbigin in *Missions in Christ's Way* tells of a study he did while a missionary in India. He asked Indians who had been converted to tell him the full story of their exposure to Christianity and their eventual conversion. Many told of ten, fifteen, and twenty times they had heard the gospel, sometimes partially, sometimes more completely, before they finally accepted Christ. Yet each step had value and helped lead to the final outcome.[7]

The limits of our discussions should be modest, aimed at clear communication and understanding. Anything else is best left to God's guiding hand. The Chinese bamboo tree does not grow—or so it seems—for its first four years. Then suddenly, during the fifth year, it shoots up ninety feet in sixty days. Would you say that the bamboo tree grew in six weeks or five years?

7. Don't create your own theology—stick with God's.

Saul was a basically good king whose one fault was doing what God asked him to—but then going one step further and also doing what *he* thought would be pleasing to God. His tendency to overreach was his undoing.[8]

Decide on the goals of your conversations with those of other traditions and stick to them. Strange things happen in face-to-face meetings. A Christian committed to loving all human beings makes new friends. He likes them and wants to please them. He can be tempted to go beyond the simple presentation of the gospel in order to accommodate his new friends.

Several things help prevent this potential drift toward syncretism:
- a thorough knowledge of one's own faith;
- a firm grounding of love in that faith;
- a commitment to transform the world.

8. Be positive. Prove Christianity, don't disprove others' religion.

Paul's experience at Ephesus teaches us a valuable lesson about approaches to other religions. Certain Ephesian artisans made their living selling statues of the goddess Artemis. Paul's preaching—and the resulting converts—threatened sales of the statues. The artisans rioted and threatened harm to Paul's traveling companions and perhaps to Paul himself.

Following the advice of friends, Paul did not speak to the incensed crowd. But the city clerk quieted them by noting that Paul and his people neither robbed temples nor blasphemed the goddess. The clerk's words helped end the riot. Paul, because of his restraint, was free to preach another day, presumably to be listened to even by the artisans.[9]

Of course we must bring our Christian world view to bear on the events of the day, and some people will inevitably take offense. But it is not our duty to systematically condemn all evil and error. God will deal with spiritual lawlessness. We must be positive, and thus gain the best hearing we can.

9. Be humble.

The Bible often tells what happens when the pride of humanity overrides the humility of creatureliness. The Tower of Babel, the Israelites' defeat at Ai, the Pharisees' legendary confidence in the Law, and the theological sinfulness that Paul describes in Romans 3 all testify to the futility of this core sin of pride.

Paul placed humility high on his list. He came to his tasks "in weakness and fear," and so should we. Talking with Hindus, Buddhists, and Muslims should involve self-criticism, a willingness to take a hard, honest look at where the practice of our faith falls far short of the ideal. Richard Mouw calls this honesty being absolutist without being overabsolutist. That's a good phrase.[10]

Or as William Wilberforce said, "The aim of the true Christian concerning his reputation before the world is like that of the Jewish ruler, of whom it was said, 'We find no fault nor occasion against this Daniel—except concerning the law of his God' (Dan. 6:5). If he gives offense, it will only be where he cannot do but otherwise."[11]

There really is no other way to approach the tremendous task of transforming the world.

Singleness of purpose

In his classic work, *An Actor Prepares*, Konstantin Stanislavski tells of an exercise he put all young actors through. "Let us do a little play," he said. "This is the plot. The curtain goes up and you are sitting on the stage. You are alone. You sit and sit and sit. At last the curtain comes down again. That is the whole play."

Stanislavski then tells what happened when his actors attempted to perform this skit. Total awkwardness was the result. One person described his feelings: "Part of me sought to entertain the onlookers so that they would not become bored; another part told me to pay no attention to them. I looked and turned stupid, funny, embarrassed, guilty, and apologetic."

After the exercise, Stanislavski gathered his young actors around him and told them why they felt so awkward. "Whatever happens on the stage must be for a purpose. Even keeping your seat must be for a purpose—a specific purpose, not just merely the general purpose of being in sight of the audience. One must earn one's right to be sitting there and it is not easy."[12]

What is the lesson for the larger stage of life—of Christian life? In order to avoid total awkwardness, we must measure everything against a single purpose. That purpose is to transform the world for Christ's sake. It is only when we have that basic purpose straight that the other niceties of life fit in.

Chapter 10

EVANGELICAL PLURALISM

I t is possible to view the dramatic increase in the world religions as a threat. Many people do. Some see it as threatening Christianity itself. Muslims, Buddhists, and Hindus already have proved to be able competitors for the souls of our neighbors. Will they win the battle?

Other people see the increase in world religions as a threat to the unique brand of representative democracy that has proved so successful in America. Without the underpinnings of Christian values, they say, democracy is doomed. Both arguments have some merit, and both have followers.

But neither line of reasoning is convincing. The Bible is quite clear that God will work his way in history no matter what humankind does. When Jesus Christ comes again at the end of the age, he will be greeted by the Christian church—a church that has remained a faithful custodian of the kingdom of God on earth. The world religions may be a threat to our egos and a threat to any triumphalistic views of how the Christian church should look as an institution, but they are not a threat to the Ruler of Creation.

And although it is quite true that representative democracy relies on a basic ethical underpinning, all of the great religions we have been discussing follow quite similar ethical systems, in spite of their broad theological differences. We cannot ignore the differences, of course. Such areas as sexual ethics and political philosophy have distinct divergences. But a common core of agreement can be discerned and can be used as a basis of general agreement.

It is better, perhaps, to view the world religions as a positive challenge than as a threat. When seen in this way, the world religions present an opportunity to strengthen the church and confront the world with the gospel in new and exciting ways. We should welcome any and all challenges to test the mettle of our faith. "Religion sharpens religion" might be the appropriate paraphrase for our current situation. Yahweh said, "I will use [the nations] to test Israel and see whether they will keep the way of the Lord."[1] Maybe he is doing it again.

If that is the case, then we in the United States have the perfect venue for the challenge of the world religions. Freedom is the soil in which religion grows best, where individual human beings can safely confront the most important questions of faith. We are indeed pilgrims in whatever land we find ourselves. This world is not our home; we are passing through on our way to heaven. Yet, while we are here we are called to transform this world as best as we can. If we must be pilgrims, erecting temporary witnesses to God's gracious work in history, we can find no better place to do it than in a nation that allows that kind of witness unencumbered by state religions and excessive bureaucratic regulations.

The question for pilgrims attempting to transform the religious landscape of a pluralistic country is *How does one do it?* I have suggested that we are to meet this challenge by following the principles in the Bible, especially those drawn from the 244 biblical pluralisms we find there. In spite of diverse political and cultural situations, and in spite of a changing landscape of God's purposes at different points in history, we still find running through the Bible three definite teachings regarding the challenge of the world religions: Love your neighbor, build the church, and preach the truth.

The three streams
Loving, building pure religious institutions, and witnessing are such prominent biblical themes that if we want to develop them, the problem is not in finding material in the Bible to draw from, but in selecting the material appropriate to the subject at hand. In addition to the biblical material, thousands of books by the best minds in Christian history have been written about each of these subjects.

A second difficulty comes with trying to integrate scriptural mandates in a consistent theological system. We have already seen how these three tenets may appear sometimes to conflict. What happens, for example, when the command to love our neighbor conflicts with the command to maintain the purity of the church? Can we really love people bent on stealing our members? Are there times when the safety of the church may inhibit the honest, energetic preaching of the gospel?

When we encounter such conflicts, there is an almost irresistible urge to unify the apparently divergent streams under one principle. This drive to unify is a natural consequence of our desire to think logically and holistically. The process of theorizing is itself built on this dynamic: reducing a wealth of collected data to their lowest common denominators, and then predicting and projecting from those bedrock principles. Einstein's great contribution, for example, was to reduce all of macrophysics to a single equation: $E = MC^2$. From that principle, Einstein thought, all else could be derived.

The same dynamic also can be effective in theology. Luther made a singular contribution to the church by taking a bewildering hodgepodge of salvation "data," including apparently conflicting church pronouncements on the question of how people are saved, and reducing it to one phrase: justification by grace alone through faith. From that principle came the Western Protestant church tradition.

Sometimes, however, the urge to simplify can be counterproductive. Often it is used as a dodge to avoid the hard implications of a spiritual truth. Church business meetings, for example, too often use prayer to avoid the hard work of resolving real differences. Obedience to God, too, is sometimes used to justify otherwise indefensible behavior. The phrase "God told me to do it" has struck fear into many a church leader's heart, because it usually comes from a person determined to start a ministry that is theologically unsound or practically impossible. Since prayer and obedience are such important, all-encompassing spiritual truths, they can be misused to paper over inconsistencies in doctrine, ethics, and everyday Christian living.

We live in an imperfect world; thus, we must live out what appear to be conflicting truths. Actually, it is not the truths themselves that conflict but the arena in which they are played that makes them seem to conflict. It is a little like hitting a beautiful, high golf shot that starts out straight for the green. But then a gust of wind comes along and blows it into the sand trap. There was nothing wrong with the pure shot, but the impure conditions strained the beauty of the effort.

Loving neighbors, building churches, and witnessing to the truth are all straightforward biblical principles. Yet putting them together in a consistent pattern can be difficult. Coordinating these three streams of biblical truth is a bit like harmonizing the checks and balances of our government. All three are essential to the smooth functioning of our system. But none can be elevated at the expense of the others, or else a dangerous imbalance of power results.

In the 1960s, for example, it became fashionable to elevate love to preeminent status in Christian living. A generation of young people, disillusioned by the hypocrisy and cynicism of their adult role models, rightly saw in Christian love an antidote to an impersonal secularism sweeping the country. Their elevation of love took two forms: the Jesus people and relational theology. At heart, however, the message was the same: All we need is love.

Unfortunately, love—at least as practiced by fallen human beings—is not big enough to fulfill this role. When love is turned into an absolute principle, it can actually become cruel. When love dictates tolerance of all people (as it should), the natural tendency is to become tolerant of more than just people, but also false ideas, destructive behavior, and a watered-down version of mission. All of these excesses happened to at least some of those sixties movements.

We discovered we need love—but love is not all we need.

It is also possible to place the well-being of the institutional church above all other concerns. Church growth has been a growth industry for several generations in the United States. Our genius for management has been transferred to the church, with some good and some bad results. On the good side of the ledger, we have seen a strong, independent-church movement arise to balance at least part of the denominational demise of the second half of the twentieth century. Largely as a result, church attendance in this country is among the highest in the world.

On the bad side of the ledger, we have seen what can happen when the institution becomes more important than the individuals who constitute the institution. This misplaced value was the primary problem the sixteenth-century Reformers faced with the church at Rome. Structures, finances, and bureaucracy had replaced spiritual well-being as the standard against which success was measured, and Martin Luther, for one, rebelled. Today we are in danger of idealizing the well-managed church. Spiritual growth and disciple-ship cannot be measured on monthly budget monitors. Institutions tend to magnify the faults of individuals not in control and idealize the strengths of individuals who are in control. Misuse of power and triumphalism result when institutional health becomes the ruling priority.

When witness becomes the dominating motif, fanaticism is the danger into which even the best-intentioned Christians can fall. The most notorious example, of course, is the Inquisition. Ortho-doxy can be a useful standard against which to measure current practice and new ideas; it can also become a rack whereby all contrary voices, good and bad, can be silenced. Stagnation and regression characterize a Christianity that sees nothing but the ideals of the faith.

People live by more than ideals. Intellectualized principles cannot do justice to the full range of the gospel. The Good News confronts more than the head of man; it demands assent from the mind, but *also* allegiance from the heart. Men and women need to be con-vinced, but they must also be wooed.

Each of the principles we have identified is important, but none of the three can be elevated over the other two. In the nitty-gritty of everyday Christian living, all three must be held in a careful balance. We must live with the tension of the situation.

What's left to do?
In facing the challenge of the world religions, more work needs to be done in each of these three areas. We know the principle and we must apply them to the specific needs of twenty-first-century America.

Ironically, the place to start searching is not current life, but biblical detail. Principles must be re-exegeted from Scripture in the context of the challenge of world religions. For example, of the ninety-two biblical pluralisms that ended in conflict, seventy-two occurred when the people of God were in a theocracy or the early monarchy. Of the forty-six biblical pluralisms that ended in cooperation, only twenty-one happened when the people of God were under a theocracy or monarchy. Apparently, being in political control does not solve the problems of confronting other religions.

Or consider the results when different kinds of world views were confronting the people of God. When the other party's religion was Philistine or Canaanite, conflicts superseded cooperations by a three-to-one margin. When the other party's religion was Hittite or Iranian, cooperations were dominant by a four-to-one margin.

Can these data help us in determining what kinds of alien ideas are most offensive to God and dangerous for Christians? Can they also help determine different approaches we should take with other faiths, depending upon the nature of their doctrines?

As we consider these crucial biblical data, theologians need to work actively to systematize them according to the specific problems and cultural situations of the day. Theologies written under the assumptions of a Christian majority are no longer useful. They must be written assuming the conditions of religious pluralism.

Only trained theologians can take the "theological facts" of current living—religious pluralism, law-mandated freedom of religion, the Great Commandment, the Great Commission, the marketplace of the faiths—and develop a consistent approach to the challenge of the world religions. This theology must go beyond the restricted theologies of internal Christian systems and articulate as never before a full Christian public philosophy. The theologian who fully incorporates these factors will be America's theologian of the twenty-first century.

Finally, practical programs of interaction with the world religions must be worked out. How are we to reach out? is the final "what to do" question, and in many ways the most important. Some work is already being done:

● When a Hindu temple was being built only blocks away from his church, Pastor Riggs taught Sunday school classes about basic Hindu beliefs. He also preached on the Christian's public and private duties in response to their new neighbors.

● When Don Lake met some Muslims through business contacts, he arranged to have them visit his church and observe a worship service.

● Many church youth groups visit services of other religious traditions to find out what they believe and how those beliefs are similar to, and differ from, their own.

● Well-written books and Sunday school curriculums are being developed to present the total religious picture of the world in which we live.

● More and more evangelism-training classes suggest different approaches for different world views, offering questions that will both interest and educate adherents of other faiths.

● Sermons are being preached on Christian responsibilities to non-Christians, recognizing that the world in which we live is no longer homogeneously Christian.

● A wealth of social-science data is available on demographic trends and the value systems that surround us. More and more religious-studies departments in colleges and universities, both Christian and secular, are conducting studies.

The goal

In chapter 65 in the Book of Isaiah, the prophet describes a model of what he sees coming for the people of God. He calls it the new heaven and new earth. The new earth, Isaiah says, will be a good place to live. People will be happy and live long lives. They will enjoy good food and have productive jobs. There will be peace: "The wolf and the lamb will feed together." We have a picture here of a world moving toward peace and harmony, built largely on the people of

God's desire to be fully obedient to God's will.

That picture, it seems, should be the goal of our relationships with people of other faiths. We must work to build the kingdom of God. But the kingdom is not a fortress. The kingdom is a well-functioning witness to God's love and purpose, influencing every part of every culture. "Thy will be done" means a church that exists to glorify God to every person and nation on earth. That is our goal; its challenge meets us today as we encounter the religious pluralism of modern America.

Appendix 1

HINDUISM

History

2000 B.C. The substratum of Hinduism was the Indus Valley religion in northwest India, much of what is modern Pakistan. It was centered in two principal cities, Mohenjo-Daro and Harapa, and characterized by cultic bathing, ritual purity, and cultic interest in fertility.

1500 B.C. A race called Aryans overran the Indus Valley civilization and established Vedism. The principal features were writings called the Vedas and the Samhitas. The Vedas established the fundamental principles of Hinduism. It gave a social organizing principle that ultimately became the caste system, was extremely polytheistic, and paid detailed attention to ritual pacification of the gods.

500 B.C. The writings of the Upanishads demythologized, to some extent, Vedic polytheism and ordered the gods under one principle, which was characterized by an interiorization and universalization of the *meaning* of the sacrifice.

A.D. *500.* Classical Hinduism established the principal doctrines of modern Hinduism and made the distinction between Śruti and Smrti.

A.D. *1700.* Reformed Hinduism arose when the pressures of nationalism and modernity confronted the ancient Hindu beliefs. Several Hindu writers began to attempt to modernize ancient beliefs without rejecting altogether the teachings of the Vedas.

Basic doctrines

Brahman. Brahman is the one universal principle of truth. All the gods are manifestations of this truth. Hinduism is basically monistic or semimonistic, which means it does not hold to a distinction between the Creator and the created or between God and humanity. Reality is one; we are all part of God; salvation consists in recognizing that fact.

Dharma. All of existence as we know it operates according to a principle of dharma or law. No one can escape dharma. The key to successful living is becoming tuned in to one's own dharma and then faithfully living it.

Samsâra. Samsâra is reality as we know it. It includes right and wrong, and human perception. Although this perception of reality is not ultimate reality, we all must live in samsâra for many lifetimes. Thus, we need to know how to identify the good and eliminate the bad.

Karma. Karma is the inexorable law of right and wrong. Successful living means doing the good that adds good karma and eliminating the bad, thereby subtracting bad karma. All deeds have an inevitable result. Good deeds bring good fruit, bad deeds bring bad fruit—if not in this life, then in a future life. Bad deeds can affect the kind of life one is born into in the next life.

Moksha. The "salvation" of Hinduism is better translated as release or liberation from this worldly life *(samsâra)* into the ultimate monistic state in which there is neither right nor wrong, positive nor negative, absolute nor mundane. It is total identification with Brahman.

Practices
Bhakti is Hindu devotion to one of the many gods, each a particular manifestation of Brahman. In practice, Hindus identify with one god as their personal god of worship.

The Four Goals define the Hindu lifestyle all men and women attempt to live. The goals are: material happiness, loving and being loved, doing one's duty, and working to achieve liberation.

The Castes of Hinduism are four: priest, warrior or leader, worker or merchant, and servant. A fifth group of people, outcastes, are outside the system with no caste rights whatsoever.

The Four Stages of life through which a Hindu passes are the roles of student when training is accomplished; householder when one earns a living and provides for a family; forest dweller when one leaves family after one has provided for them adequately and attempts to learn religious wisdom; and renouncer when wisdom is achieved at a certain level and all material goods are renounced.

Six Philosophies explain how liberation *(moksha)* is achieved. Intellectually oriented Hindus might choose one of these philosophies to follow.

Demographics
Hinduism is a religion of 80 percent of the population of India, which is 700 million people. Recent estimates of the number of Hindus worldwide put it at approximately 650 million. Most Hindus live in India. However, Hinduism has a growing presence in the United States. Some of the forms of exported Hinduism that have

taken root in America include: the Vedanta Society, the Self-Realization Fellowship, the International Society for Krishna Consciousness (Hare Krishnas), Transcendental Meditation (TM), and the Divine Light Mission.

Appendix 2

BUDDHISM

History

563–483 B.C. These dates are traditionally given for the life of the Buddha in northeast India.

483–270 B.C. The age of the councils followed the Buddha's death, during which Buddhist teaching was standardized.

270 B.C.–A.D. 100. The age of Asoka is named after the first political figure to wholeheartedly adopt Buddhism. Asoka, an Indian king, encouraged the teaching of Buddhist principles in India, and he also sent missionaries to surrounding countries to spread the doctrine.

A.D. 100–900. During the age of expansion, Buddhism spread south to Sri Lanka, east to Thailand, Burma, and Vietnam, and north to China, Tibet, and Japan.

A.D. 900–1600. Assimilation marked Buddhism when it adapted itself to each of the countries to which it had spread, taking on a unique form and at the same time maintaining the essential core doctrines common to all Buddhists.

A.D. 1600–present. During the modern age, Buddhism has become a worldwide religion spreading to Europe and the United States.

Basic doctrines

Buddha. The word literally means "enlightened one" and describes one who has become fully aware of the way things are. There have been numerous Buddhas, but it was Gautama Buddha (ca. 563–483 B.C.) who left us the current teaching.

Dukkha. The first truth of the four noble truths of Buddhism teaches that everything about our current existence is suffering (dukkha). Even the good things that happen to us are temporary. The enlightened person is one who fully realizes that sorrow pervades all of life.

Paticca-samuppada. The cycle of conditioned existence teaches that anything that happens is conditioned by something else, and events recur in cyclical patterns. The secret to coping with this suffering existence is to break out of the circle of conditioned existence that leads to endless rebirths.

Magga. The path that leads to a realization of the truth of suffering is called the noble eightfold path. It is the ethical component of Buddhism. The path consists of right views, right thoughts, right speech, right conduct, right livelihood, right effort, right mindfulness, and right meditation.

Anicca/Anatta. Anicca is the teaching that everything is impermanent and will pass away. Anatta is the teaching that even the self is impermanent, and there is no ongoing personal entity that lasts from life to life. Buddhists do believe in rebirth, but they make it consistent with the doctrine of anatta by using the analogy of a flame being passed from one candle to another. Nothing about the person goes from one life to the next, but a continuity of some kind passes along.

Nirvana. The state one enters when one becomes fully enlightened is called Nirvana.

Major schools
Theravāda, the way of the elders, is the oldest, most conservative and literal-minded about the original Buddhist teachings. Adherents of this school attempt to live ethical lives, support the community of monks, and revere the memory and teaching (Dhamma) of the Buddha. They are particularly well-known for insight meditation techniques, which have become features of Theravāda Buddhist groups in the United States.

Mahāyāna is the form Buddhism took in China, Japan, and East Asia. It took the original teachings of the Buddha and added the *bodhisattva* ideal, which teaches that there are many Buddhas living in Buddha heavens who can help people in various ways along the path to enlightenment.

Vajrayāna is Tibetan Buddhism developed as an esoteric and instinct-oriented version of Buddhism. The emphasis is on the guru-disciple relationship, stressing immediate and sudden enlightenment with the aid of *mandalas* (visual meditative aids) and *mantras* (repetitive meditation keys that aid in insight).

Zen is one of the forms Buddhism took in Japan. It is a meditative version of Buddhism where one attempts to get beyond the good/evil, conditioned duality of this existence through the use of *koans* or phrases that go beyond mundane logic. The early history of United States Buddhism was largely Zen oriented.

Demographics
Currently it is estimated that there are 300 million Buddhists worldwide. Forms of Buddhism in the United States include all the

major sects, Theravāda, Mahāyāna (including Zen, both Rinzai and Soto), and Vajrayāna. In addition, several export forms of Buddhism, particularly from Japan, include Buddhist Churches of America (Pure Land), Nichiren Shoshu, and various Tibetan groups.

Appendix 3

ISLAM

History

A.D. 610. Muhammad received the Qur'an.

A.D. 622. Muhammad took flight from Mecca to Medina; the date is usually considered the official beginning of Islam as a religion.

A.D. 650. The Sunnī, Shī'ite, and Khārijite factions of the tradition split over arguments about who were the proper heirs to Muhammad's leadership.

A.D. 715–1500. Islam rapidly spread throughout the Middle East, and from there to North Africa, Spain, India, Central Asia, and Constantinople.

A.D. *1800–1970*. Islam was confronted with Western ways of thinking and was politically dominated by European countries. Islamic countries attempted to deal with the impact of Western culture in three ways: Reform the tradition to adapt to modernity (e.g., Qaddafi in Libya); secularize the tradition, splitting the religious from the political (e.g., Ataturk in Turkey); or return to the fundamentalist tradition (e.g., Khomeini in Iran).

A.D. *1970 to present*. Modern Islam has experienced a revival of fundamentalist characteristics and strength. Two reasons are the large amounts of money brought by petroleum products and the decline of Western ability to control the world's thinking.

Basic doctrines

God (Allāh). Absolute monotheism is the theology of those who believe in the God of Abraham, Isaac, Jacob, Jesus, and Muhammad.

Angels. These beings live in spiritual realm and act as God's agents.

Books. Principally they are the Qur'an. The Jewish and Christian Scriptures, as they were originally given by God, are also included; current versions are said to have been corrupted by Jews and Christians.

Prophets. Twenty-eight prophets are mentioned in the Qur'an, most of them biblical figures. Muhammad is the most important, the final messenger.

Day of Judgment. All humankind will be judged at the end of history.

Predestination. The will of God determines everything that happens. Since Muslims also believe in man having some free will, the debate between the two positions in Islam in some ways parallels that in Christianity.

Practices

The Five Pillars are the practices every Muslim must follow and that define an adherent of the tradition: (1) Faith *(īmān)* is assent to the *shahādah:* "There is no God but Allah and Muhammad is his prophet"; (2) Prayer *(salah)* is observed five times daily (dawn, noon, afternoon, sunset, and night); (3) Fasting *(sawm)* means no eating from dawn to sunset during the month of Ramadan; (4) Alms *(zakāh)* are given to the needy; (5) Pilgrimage *(hajj)* to Mecca is made at least once in the life of a devout Muslim financially able to afford it.

Strict Morality is a hallmark of Muslims. There are strong prohibitions against drinking wine, eating pork, gambling, practicing usury, and wearing gold or silk.

Holy War (jihād) means a strong impetus to defend the Islamic community and also defend one's own faith in both a literal and a figurative sense.

Missions (dawah) to non-Muslims means Muslims are expected to spread the faith worldwide. The call to Islam is a growing feature of Islam in the United States.

The Law (shari'a) encompasses not only religion and morality but all of culture, politics, and economics. Thus, in a fundamentalist Muslim country there is no difference between the political realm and the religious realm. Clerics are politicians and politicians are clerics.

Demographics
There are approximately 900 million Muslims worldwide, 17 percent of the world's population. In the United States, the best estimates put the figure at three million Muslims. Principal organizations include the Federation of Islamic Associations and the Islamic Society of North America. American Muslims tend to downplay the Sunnī- and Shī'ite-sect distinction in favor of a more homogenized version of the basic faith.

Appendix 4

BIBLICAL PLURALISMS

Incidents
1. Genesis 3:1–24: Serpent confronts Adam and Eve.
2. Genesis 6:1–22: Intermarriage between good and evil partners.
3. Genesis 11:1–9: The Tower of Babel.
4. Genesis 12:10–20: Abram in Egypt.
5. Genesis 14: Abram rescues Lot, confronts Melchizedek.
6. Genesis 16:1–16: Hagar and Ishmael (also 21:8–20).
7. Genesis 19: Lot and Sodom.
8. Genesis 20—21: Abraham and Abimelech.
9. Genesis 23: Abraham buys land from the Hittites.
10. Genesis 26: Isaac and Abimelech.
11. Genesis 24:29–31:55: Jacob and Laban.

12. Genesis 34: Dinah and Shechem.
13. Genesis 38: Judah and Tamar.
14. Genesis 39–41: Joseph and Egyptians.
15. Genesis 50: Joseph embalms dead father.
16. Exodus 1–15: Israelites and Egyptians.
17. Exodus 17:8–16: Israelites and Amalekites.
18. Exodus 32: The golden calf (Deut. 9:7–29).
19. Leviticus 24:10–23: A blasphemer stoned.
20. Numbers 20:14–21: Edom denies Israel passage.
21. Numbers 21:1–3: Israelites destroy Arad.
22. Numbers 21:21–35: Defeat of Amorites (King Sihon).
23. Numbers 22–24: Israelites and Moabites (King Balak).
24. Numbers 25: Israelites and Moabite women.
25. Joshua 2: Rahab.
26. Joshua 5–6: The battle of Jericho.
27. Joshua 7–8: Ai defeats Israel.
28. Joshua 9: The Gibeonites' ruse.
29. Joshua 10:1–28: Five Amorite kings killed.
30. Joshua 10:29–43: Joshua destroys southern cities.
31. Joshua 11: Joshua destroys northern cities.
32. Judges 1: The Canaanite campaign.
33. Judges 2:6–3:5: Baal and Ashtoreths.
34. Judges 3:7–11: Othniel and Aramites.
35. Judges 3:12–31: Ehud and Moabites.
36. Judges 4: Deborah.
37. Judges 6–8: Gideon.
38. Judges 8:33–35: Israel worships Baal.
39. Judges 10:6–12:7: Jephthah.
40. Judges 13–16: Samson and the Philistines.
41. Judges 17–18: Micah's idols.
42. Ruth 1: Naomi and Ruth.
43. 1 Samuel 4–6: Philistines capture the Ark.
44. 1 Samuel 7:2–17: Samuel subdues the Philistines.
45. 1 Samuel 11:1–11: Saul and the city of Jabesh.
46. 1 Samuel 13–14: Saul, Jonathan, and Philistines.
47. 1 Samuel 15: Saul defeats Amalekites but disobeys God.
48. 1 Samuel 17: David and Goliath.
49. 1 Samuel 23:1–6: David saves Keilah.

50. 1 Samuel 27: David's raiders.
51. 1 Samuel 28: Philistines defeat Saul.
52. 1 Samuel 30: David destroys Amalekites.
53. 2 Samuel 1:1–16: David kills Amalekite messenger.
54. 2 Samuel 5:6–10: David captures Jerusalem from Jebusites.
55. 2 Samuel 5:11–12: David and Hiram.
56. 2 Samuel 5:17–25: David defeats Philistines.
57. 2 Samuel 8:1–14: Philistines, Moabites, Arameans, and Edomites.
58. 2 Samuel 10:1–4: David and Hanun.
59. 2 Samuel 12:26–31: Rabbah of the Ammonites.
60. 2 Samuel 15:19–22: Ittai the Gittite.
61. 2 Samuel 21:1–14: David settles with the Gibeonites.
62. 2 Samuel 21:15–22: Wars against the Philistines.
63. 1 Kings 5: Solomon and Hiram.
64. 1 Kings 9:10–28: Solomon's treatment of foreigners.
65. 1 Kings 10:1–13: Solomon and the Queen of Sheba.
66. 1 Kings 11:1–13: Solomon's wives.
67. 1 Kings 11:14–25: Solomon's adversaries.
68. 1 Kings 14:21–28: Rehoboam (Judah) and Shishak (Egypt).
69. 1 Kings 15:9–22: Asa and Ben-Hadad.
70. 1 Kings 17:7–24: Elijah and the widow at Zarephath.
71. 1 Kings 18:16–45: Elijah and the prophets of Baal.
72. 1 Kings 20:1–43: Ahab and Ben Hadad.
73. 1 Kings 21:17–28: Ahab and Jezebel.
74. 1 Kings 22:29–38: Ahab and Jehoshaphat.
75. 1 Kings 22:46: Jehoshaphat and male shrine prostitutes.
76. 1 Kings 22:52–53: Ahaziah serves Baal.
77. 2 Kings 1:1–18: Elijah and Ahaziah.
78. 2 Kings 3: Moab revolts.
79. 2 Kings 5:1–18: Elisha heals Naaman's leprosy.
80. 2 Kings 6:8–23: Elisha traps blinded Arameans.
81. 2 Kings 6:24–7:20: Ben-Hadad and Arameans besiege Samaria.
82. 2 Kings 8:7–15: Hazael murders Ben-Hadad.
83. 2 Kings 8:20–22: Edom and Libnah revolt against Israel.
84. 2 Kings 8:25–29: Joram wounded in battle against Hazael.
85. 2 Kings 10:18–35: Jehu destroys prophets and temple of Baal.

86. 2 Kings 12:17–21: Joash pays off Hazael.
87. 2 Kings 13:1–7, 22–25: Israel under subjection to Aram.
88. 2 Kings 14:7: Amaziah defeats Edomites in Valley of Salt.
89. 2 Kings 15:19–20: Menahem pays Pul tribute.
90. 2 Kings 15:29: Assyria invades Israel and deports many.
91. 2 Kings 16:1–18: Assyrians aid Judah.
92. 2 Kings 17:1–23: Assyria totally defeats Israel.
93. 2 Kings 18:17—37: Sennacherib threatens Jerusalem.
94. 2 Kings 20:12–21: Hezekiah and envoys from Babylon.
95. 2 Kings 21:1–16: Manasseh and Amon erect altars to Baal.
96. 2 Kings 22; 23:1–28: Josiah restores Book of the Law.
97. 2 Kings 23:29–30: Pharaoh kills Josiah.
98. 2 Kings 23:31–35: Pharaoh Neco enchains Jehoahaz.
99. 2 Kings 23:36–24:6: Jehoiakim a vassal of Babylon.
100. 2 Kings 24:8–17: Nebuchadnezzar besieges Jerusalem.
101. 2 Kings 25:1–26: Nebuchadnezzar devastates Judah.
102. 2 Chronicles 14:8–15: Asa battles Zerah, the Cushite.
103. 2 Chronicles 20:1–30: The Lord defeats the Moabites and Ammonites.
104. 2 Chronicles 20:16–17: Philistines and Arabs plunder Judah.
105. 2 Chronicles 25:14–15: Amaziah worships idols.
106. 2 Chronicles 26:6–8: Uzziah defeats Philistines.
107. 2 Chronicles 27:5: Jotham defeats Ammonites.
108. 2 Chronicles 36:22–23: Cyrus allows rebuilding of temple.
109. Ezra 3:7: Sidon and Tyre bring materials to build temple.
110. Ezra 4:1–5: Enemies frustrate rebuilding of temple.
111. Ezra 4:6–24: Trans-Euphrates frustrate rebuilding of temple.
112. Ezra 6:1–15: The decree of King Darius.
113. Ezra 7:11–28: King Artaxerxes' letter to Ezra.
114. Nehemiah 2, 4, 6: Sanballat, Tobiah, Geshem oppose Nehemiah.
115. Nehemiah 5:1–13: Nehemiah stops practice of usury.
116. Esther 2:19–23: Mordecai uncovers plot against Xerxes.
117. Jeremiah 29:1–23: Nebuchadnezzar kills false prophets.
118. Jeremiah 38:7–13: Ebed-Melech rescues Jeremiah.
119. Jeremiah 40:1–6: Nebuzaradan releases Jeremiah from captives.
120. Jeremiah 40:7–41:15: Gedaliah murdered by Ishmael.

121. Daniel 1: Defilement with foreign gods.
122. Daniel 2: Daniel interprets Nebuchadnezzar's dream.
123. Daniel 3: Three men in a fiery furnace.
124. Daniel 4: Daniel and Nebuchadnezzar's dream.
125. Daniel 5: Belshazzar and the writing on the wall.
126. Daniel 6: Daniel in the den of lions.
127. Jonah 1:1–16: Jonah runs from God to a ship of foreigners.
128. Jonah 3–4: Nineveh repents of wickedness.
129. Matthew 2:1–12: Eastern wise men worship Jesus.
130. Acts 2:1–12: Pentecost.
131. Acts 8:1–25: Paul and Simon the Sorcerer.
132. Acts 8:26–40: Philip and the Ethiopian.
133. Acts 10: Peter's visit to Cornelius; Peter's vision.
134. Acts 15: Council's basic requirements for gentile converts.
135. Acts 17:16–34: Paul in Athens.
136. Acts 19:23–20:38: Paul and the worship of Artemis.
137. Acts 27: Paul's shipwreck on a Roman vessel.
138. Acts 28: Paul in a Roman prison.

Teachings
1. Genesis 12:1–3: The call of Abram.
2. Genesis 15:12–21: Covenant with Abram.
3. Genesis 17: God's special promise to Abram.
4. Genesis 18:16–33: Abraham pleads for Sodom.
5. Genesis 24: Intermarriage considerations (also 26, 28).
6. Exodus 22:18: Law for sorceresses.
7. Exodus 23:9: Law for aliens (also Lev. 19:33–34).
8. Exodus 23:20–33: Israelites and enemies in Promised Land.
9. Exodus 34:13: Asherah poles (or trees).
10. Deuteronomy 4:15: Idolatry forbidden.
11. Deuteronomy 20: Rules for going to war.
12. Deuteronomy 21:21; 22: Institutional purity.
13. Judges 2:1–5: The cost of ignoring God's command.
14. 1 Samuel 12: Samuel's farewell speech.
15. 1 Kings 2:2–4: David's charge to Solomon.
16. 1 Kings 8:22–53: Solomon's dedicatory prayer.
17. 1 Kings 9:6–9: God's warning to Solomon.

18. 2 Kings 19:21–34: God's prophecy and judgment on Assyria.
19. Ezra 9–10: Ezra's prayer for Israel.
20. Nehemiah 13:1–9: Reforms instituted concerning foreigners.
21. Psalm 9:2–6,13–16: God rebukes nations and destroys wicked.
22. Psalm 18:34–48: David's enemies fear him.
23. Psalm 44: Sons of Korah defeated by enemies.
24. Psalm 60:4–12: Aram and Edom defeated.
25. Psalm 74:4–8: Mocking of enemies of Asaph.
26. Psalm 83: Israel's prayer to God to crush enemies.
27. Psalm 115: Disparagement of foreign gods.
28. Psalm 135: Praise of God and disparagement of idols.
29. Isaiah 8:19–20: Warning against consulting mediums.
30. Isaiah 10:20–34: Prophecy against nations.
31. Isaiah 13–14:23: Prophecy against many nations.
32. Isaiah 30:1–5: Woe to those who turn to Egypt rather than God.
33. Isaiah 44:6–23: Isaiah preaches against idolatry.
34. Isaiah 56:3–8: Salvation for all who serve the Lord.
35. Jeremiah 1:11–19: Disaster because of idolatry.
36. Jeremiah 22:1–9: Judgment against evil kings.
37. Jeremiah 25:15–38: God's wrath against all nations.
38. Jeremiah 41:16–44:30: Prophecy about idolatry in Egypt.
39. Jeremiah 46–51: Prophecy against nations.
40. Lamentations 1:3, 5, 7–10: Judah in exile.
41. Lamentations 2:7, 15–18: Lament over destruction of Jerusalem.
42. Lamentations 4:12–13: Lament over destruction of Jerusalem.
43. Lamentations 5:6: Submission to Egypt and Assyria.
44. Ezekiel 11:16–25: Judgment of foreign nations.
45. Ezekiel 21:28–32: Prophecy about several foreign nations.
46. Hosea 8:8–10: Israel sells herself to idolatry.
47. Joel 3: Nations judged.
48. Amos: Judgment of Israel and neighbors.
49. Obadiah: Prophecy about Edom.
50. Micah 4:2–5: Many nations to worship God.
51. Nahum: Prophecy of fall of Nineveh.
52. Zephaniah 1:4–6: Prophecy concerning idolatry.

53. Zephaniah 2: Prophecy about five nations.
54. Zechariah 9:1–8: Judgment on Israel's enemies.
55. Malachi 2:11–12: Foreign marriages and idolatry.
56. Matthew 5:43–48: Jesus' command to love enemies.
57. Matthew 6:5–6: Praying in private.
58. Matthew 6:7–8: Command not to pray like pagans.
59. Matthew 7:1–5: Command not to judge others.
60. Matthew 7:6: Command not to cast pearls before swine.
61. Matthew 7:15–20: Fruits of spiritual life.
62. Matthew 8:5–13: Faith of a centurion.
63. Matthew 10: 5–42: Behavioral model for Christians.
64. Matthew 13:24–30: Wheat and tares parable.
65. Matthew 15:13–20: False teaching.
66. Matthew 18:1–14: Command to act correctly so that others won't sin.
67. Matthew 22:36–40: Two greatest commandments.
68. Matthew 24: False teachers.
69. Matthew 25:14–30: Parable of talents.
70. Matthew 26:59–64: Hostile questions.
71. Matthew 28:18–20: Great Commission.
72. Mark 3:24–27: Understanding our belief.
73. Mark 9:50: Being salt in the world.
74. Luke 2:44–50: Jesus in the temple.
75. Luke 10:25–37: Good Samaritan.
76. Luke 12:49–53: Jesus does not bring peace.
77. Luke 18:9–14: Self-righteousness.
78. Luke 24:46–49: Preaching in Christ's name.
79. John 2:12–23: Jesus clears the temple.
80. John 15:1–8: The vine and the branches.
81. John 15:18–16:4: Hate for the followers of Jesus.
82. Romans 1–2: All men are sinners.
83. Romans 3: Righteousness comes through faith.
84. Romans 12: Love in Christianity is a special kind of attitude.
85. Romans 13: Obedience to authority.
86. Romans 14: Acting so the weak do not stumble.
87. 1 Corinthians 2:1–5: Humility.
88. 1 Corinthians 8: Love is superior to knowledge.
89. 1 Corinthians 10:1–22: Good versus evil.

90. 1 Corinthians 10:23–33: Food offered to idols.
91. 1 Corinthians 13: Love.
92. 1 Corinthians 16: Institution, ideas, and individuals.
93. 2 Corinthians 4: Simplicity of the gospel.
94. 2 Corinthians 6:14–18: Yoked with unbelievers.
95. Galatians 5:22–23: Fruit of the Spirit.
96. Philippians 2:1–11: Imitating Christ's humility.
97. Colossians 2:16–17: Reality in Christ.
98. 2 Thessalonians 2:5–12: Contention.
99. Titus 3:9–11: Foolish controversies.
100. 1 Peter 4:8: Love.
101. 2 Peter 2: False teachers.
102. 1 John 2:18: Antichrists.
103. 1 John 3:11–24: Love for one another.
104. 1 John 4: Testing the spirits.
105. Jude 4: Godless men among believers.
106. Jude 21–23: Putting love to work.

NOTES

Chapter 1: The Invisible Crisis

1. *Statistics of the Population of the United States at the 10th Census* (Washington, D.C.: Government Printing Office, 1883), 12, 34. *The 1970 Census of Population* (Washington, D.C.: The Bureau of the Census, 1970), 262.

2. "Religion," in *Harvard Encyclopedia of American Ethnic Groups* (Cambridge: Harvard University Press, 1980), 869.

3. *Encyclopedia of American Religions* (Detroit: Gale Research, 1989).

4. Survey by Christianity Today, Inc., research department, summer 1988.

5. *Emerging Trends 9*, No. 2 (1984), 3.

6. See "Characteristics of the Population," Part 1, U.S. Summary, *Census of the Population 1970 1* (Washington, D.C., U.S. Bureau of the Census, 1973), 103, table 97.

7. "Many Urban Problems Found Worse in 1988," *New York Times* (Jan. 13, 1989), 3.

8. Cheryl McCall, "To Keep a Cult from Taking Over, an Oregon Town Wants to Go Out of Business," *People Weekly* (April 19, 1982), 123–25.

9. *Aurora* (Ill.) *Beacon News*, various stories from fall 1983.

10. Michael Barone and Grant Ujifusa, *The Almanac of American Politics, 1988* (Washington, D.C.: National Journal, 1988).

11. David Rosenthal, "The Asian Few: A Growing Minority Still Goes Mostly Unrepresented on TV," *Chicago Tribune* (May 6, 1989), 16.

12. See "Ethnic Churches—Where Are They Going?" *Christianity Today* (March 3, 1989), 25–42, for a discussion of how the various ethnic groups have fared in the U.S. economy.

13. For a discussion of how Islam is faring in this task, see Yvonne Haddad and Adair Lummis, *Islamic Values in the United States* (New York: Oxford University Press, 1987). See also Martin E. Marty, *Pilgrims in Their Own Land: 500 Years of Religion in America* (Boston: Little, Brown, 1984), 444–47.

14. *Church and State in the United States* (New York: Harper & Brothers, 1950), 24.

15. David Barrett, *World Christian Encyclopedia* (New York: Oxford University Press, 1982).

Chapter 2: New Neighbors

1. It would be roughly analogous to the inclusion of Mormons, Jehovah's Witnesses, and Christian Scientists in the figures for Christianity. For some purposes it might be accurate to include such groups. For others it is not.

2. Yvonne Haddad and Adair Lummis, *Islamic Values in the United States* (New York: Oxford University Press, 1987), 13–14.

3. Edwin Gaustad, *A Documentary History of Religion in America Since 1865* (Grand Rapids: Eerdmans, 1983), 547–49.

4. See Terry Muck, "The Mosque Next Door," *Christianity Today* (Feb. 19, 1988), 15–20.

5. Kent Hart, "Islam in America," *Theology News and Notes* (Dec. 1988), 6–9.

6. E. Allen Richardson, *East Comes West* (New York: Pilgrim Press, 1985), 16–26. See also John Fenton, "Hinduism," in *Encyclopedia of the American Religious Experience* (New York: Charles Scribner's Sons, 1988), 683–98.

7. Shundra Bose, "Travelling Through the Country in America," *Modern Review 9* (Jan. 1911), 251.

8. Rick Fields, *How the Swans Came to the Lake: A Narrative History of Buddhism in America* (Boulder, Colo.: Shambhala Press), 98. Other studies of the growth and status of Buddhism in America include Emma McCloy Layman, *Buddhism in America* (Chicago: Nelson-Hall, 1976), and Charles Prebish, *American Buddhism* (Belmont, Calif.: Duxbury Press, 1979).

9. "Profile of Tomorrow's New United States," *U.S. News & World Report* (December 24, 1986), 32; "U.S. Could Become a Nation of Minorities," *The Futurist* (March/April 1986), 57.

10. Gordon Melton, *The Encyclopedia of American Religions* (Detroit: Gale Research, 1989), xliv.

11. Martin E. Marty, *Pilgrims in Their Own Land: 500 Years of*

Religion in America (Boston: Little, Brown, 1984), 10.

12. Robert Bellah and Fredrick Greenspahn, *Uncivil Religion: Inter-religious Hostility in America* (New York: Crossroad, 1987).

13. Already the trend is stretching traditional concepts of tolerance beyond where they may be able to go. There have been calls for strict immigration reversals to go back to the laws of the 1920s where no people would be allowed in the United States from these Asian countries (Thomas Fleming, "The Real American Dilemma," *Chronicles of Culture* [March 1989], 8–11). Others are asking for different definitions of immigrants and what they should be allowed to do in the U.S. (see Robert Pear, "Deciding Who's a Refugee," *New York Times* [Jan. 23, 1989]). But it is creating other stresses as well. Individual incidences of religious intolerance are at a five-year high. One example: Anti-Semitic incidents in the United States rose to a five-year high in 1988 as reported by the Anti-Defamation League of B'nai B'rith. Antireligious incidents against Muslims and Buddhists follow a similar curve *(New York Times* [Jan. 29, 1989]). Others are worried about interfaith marriages. In 1957, 6 percent of Americans had a spouse of a different faith. Today that number has climbed to 20 percent ("Interfaith Anxiety," *Psychology Today* [Dec. 1988], 6). The pressure to define more clearly what religious toleration means has commenced.

Chapter 3: Competing Missionaries

1. For an understanding of the Vedanta Society and their teachings, see Swami Vivekananda, *Vedanta: Voice of Freedom* (Calcutta: Advaita Ashrama, 1987).

2. Two excellent accounts of what went on at the World's Parliament of Religions are available: Richard Seager, *The World Parliament of Religions* (Cambridge: Harvard University Press, 1986); another is an unpublished dissertation at the University of Chicago by Kenten Druyvefteyn, called the *World's Parliament of Religions*, written in 1976. The proceedings and papers of the parliament were collected and published: John Barrows, *The World Parliament of Religions* (Chicago: Parliament, 1893).

3. On Vivekananda's heroic return to India, see Eric Sharpe,

Comparative Religion (LaSalle, Ill.: Open Court, 1975), 255. "He [Vivekananda] reached the ear of the Western world as Ramakrishna had never done and on his return was hailed as India's first missionary to the West. He became a national hero."

4. R. C. Zaehner, *Hinduism* (Oxford: Oxford University Press, 1962).

5. S. Arles, "Hindu Response to Pluralism," *Evangelical Review of Theology*, Vol. 12, No. 3 (July 1988), 196–207.

6. *Hinduism Today: An International Monthly Newspaper Fostering Hindu Solidarity Among 700 Million Members of a Global Religion.* Published in San Francisco, California.

7. *Introduction to Nichiren Shoshu* (Chicago: Nichiren Shoshu Temple, 1988).

8. "Mahaparinibbana Sutra," *Digha Nikaya* (London: Luzac, 1971), 112. For a concise introduction to Buddhist doctrine, see Walpola Rahula, *What the Buddha Taught* (New York: Grove Press, 1974).

9. Gordon Melton, *The Encyclopedia of American Religions* (Detroit: Gale, 1989), xlvii.

10. *Chicago Tribune* (Oct. 7, 1987), B2; *Chronicles of Higher Education* (July 29, 1987), 3.

11. Sura 16:125–26 (*Sura* means chapter. The Qur'an is divided into 114 suras.). Qur'an references are from *The Holy Qur'an*, A Yusuf Ali, trans. (Washington, D.C.: The Islamic Center, 1978).

12. Sura 2:193.

13. Rudolph Peters, "Jihad," *Encyclopedia of Religion* (New York: Macmillan, 1987).

14. Bruce Shelley, *Church History in Plain Language* (Waco, Tex.: Word Books, 1982), 193.

15. Good summaries of Islam include: Fazlur Rahman, *Islam* (Chicago: University of Chicago Press, 1979), and Kenneth Cragg, *Call of the Minaret* (Maryknoll, N.Y.: Orbis Press, 1985).

16. Kent Hart, "Islam in America," *Theology News and Notes* (Dec. 1988), 6–9.

17. The Muslims are perhaps the most systematic about this. The Washington, D.C., Islamic Center, for example, sells a series of illustrated books that teach the fundamentals of Islam in graded curriculum, called *Islamic Religious Knowledge for Religious Classes.* They also publish books and pamphlets on specific teachings and how they apply to modern issues. A few examples: *Islam in Focus;*

Essentials of Muslim Prayer; Islam and Modern Values. Biblical Studies from a Muslim Perspective; Islam and Humane Tenets. In addition, they publish three magazines: *Bulletin of the Islamic Center,* published bimonthly; *Al Nur* (the Light) published quarterly; and *Noor Ul Haq* (Light of Truth), published in Arabic.

But the Buddhists also recognize the importance of this. The Washington, D.C., Buddhist Vihara has Sunday-morning school for children of all ages, and they too publish a quarterly magazine, *The Washington Buddhist,* free to all who wish it.

The Hindus have been the least active in some ways. But the Himalayan Academy, publishers of a monthly newspaper, *Hinduism Today,* recently published a curriculum of basic Hindu beliefs aimed at a Western market of all ages, called *Hindu Catechism: The Master Course Book One.* Also advertised in the pages of the newspaper is a listing of children's schools, weekend classes, and summer camps held at various temples and ashrams around the country.

Chapter 4: Pluralism 101

1. There are several good collections of America's founding documents. See *Basic American Documents* (Ames, Iowa: Littlefield, Adams, 1953).

2. In the case of judging laws, the U.S. Supreme Court uses a three-part test to determine whether a statute satisfies the Constitution's demand for separation of church and state. Called the "Lemon Test" (after a 1971 Supreme Court decision, *Lemon v. Kurtzman*), its three points are: The statute must have a secular legislative purpose; its principal or primary effect must be one that neither advances nor inhibits religion; the statute must not foster an excessive governmental entanglement with religion.

3. C. S. Lewis, *The Abolition of Man* (New York: Macmillan, 1947), 29.

4. Alexis de Tocqueville, *Democracy in America* (Harper & Row, 1960), 295.

5. Tocqueville, 296–97.

6. N. A. Nikam and Richard McKeon, ed. and trans., *The Edicts of Asoka* (Chicago: University of Chicago Press, 1959), 51–52.

7. The following typology is modified from the one used by Anson Phelps Stokes, *Church and State in the United States*, Vol. 1 (New York: Harper & Brothers, 1950), 39ff.

8. See Norman Cousins, *In God We Trust* (New York: Harper & Brothers, 1958). Also helpful: Mark Noll, *One Nation Under God* (San Francisco: Harper & Row, 1988).

9. Will Herberg, *Protestant, Catholic, Jew: An Essay in American Religious Sociology* (Chicago: University of Chicago Press, 1960).

Chapter 5: The Problem of Transforming the World

1. H. Richard Niebuhr, *Christ and Culture* (New York: Harper & Row, 1951).

2. Ibid., 190.

3. Romans 12:2.

4. "On Faith and the Creed," *The Nicene and Post Nicene Fathers, First Series*, Vol. 3 (Grand Rapids: Eerdmans, 1978), 268ff.

5. St. Thomas Aquinas, *Summa Theologica* II–III, q. 2, Art. 5, Ad. 1; III, q. 61, Art. 1; II, q. 2, Art. 7. See *The Basic Writings of St. Thomas Aquinas*, Anton Pegis, trans. (New York: Random House, 1945).

6. "On War Against the Turk," *Works of Martin Luther*, Vol. 5 (Grand Rapids: Baker Book House, 1982), 88–89, 95–96.

7. *Institutes of the Christian Religion*, Vol. 1, John T. McNeill, ed., and Ford Lewis Battles, trans. (Philadelphia: Westminster Press, 1960), 49.

8. *Church Dogmatics*, Vol. 1/2 (Edinburgh: T. & T. Clark, 1956), 280–361.

9. See Appendix 4 for a listing of these biblical pluralisms.

10. For a discussion of some of the problems, see Elmer B. Smick, "Old Testament Cross-Culturalism: Paradigmatic or Enigmatic?" *Journal of the Evangelical Theological Society* (March 1989), 3–16.

Chapter 6: Loving Neighbors

1. Other love passages include Matthew 5:43–48; 22:36–40; Romans 12; 1 Corinthians 13; 1 Peter 4:8; 1 John 3:11–24.

2. *Emerging Trends* (March 1987), 1.

3. Bruce Shelley, *Church History in Plain Language* (Waco, Tex.: Word Books, 1982), 66.

4. *Emerging Trends* (November 1985), 1.

5. Reported in *The Church Around the World* (March 1987), 1.

6. Hendrik Kraemer, *The Christian's Message in a Non-Christian World* (New York: Harper & Brothers, 1938).

7. See Mark Horst, "The Problem with Theological Pluralism," *The Christian Century* (Nov. 5, 1986), 971ff.

8. Matthew 7:1–5.

9. 1 Corinthians 9:22b.

10. Jude 22.

11. Lesslie Newbigin, *Mission in Christ's Way* (Geneva, Switzerland: WCC, 1987), 35.

12. See Matthew 4:11; 12:15; 14:13, 23; 26:36; Mark 1:35; 7:24; and other references to Jesus' strategic withdrawals throughout the Gospels.

13. 2 Corinthians 6:14ff.

Chapter 7: The Clash of Institutions

1. See Terry Muck, "The Mosque Next Door," *Christianity Today* (Feb. 19, 1988), 15ff.

2. James Madison, *American State Papers*, in Great Books of the Western World, Vol. 43, Robert Hutchins, ed. (Chicago: Encyclopedia Britannica, 1952), 53. Martin Marty called attention to this writing.

3. Matthew 15:3–20; 7:8, 24; Luke 11:39–40; 2 Peter 2:1–22; 1 John 2:18; Jude 1; 2 Corinthians 6:14–18; Genesis 18–19, 24, 29–31; Judges 17–18; 2 Kings 10:18–35; 16:1–18; 20–21; 22; 23; 2 Chronicles 25:14–15; Daniel 1:1–21; 2 Kings 18:1–19, and other Exile passages.

4. Acts 10:9ff.

5. Matthew 7:6.

6. See, for example, Genesis 12, 20.

7. 2 Chronicles 36:22–23; Ezra 5–6; Nehemiah 2, 4, 6. For other Old Testament examples of cooperative competition see 2 Samuel

15:19–22 (David and Ittai); 1 Kings 10:1–13 (Solomon and the Queen of Sheba); 2 Kings 6:8–23; 5:1–18. Sincere Christians often have authority in front of non-Christians. See Acts 27.

8. See the following passages: 2 Samuel 5:11–12; 1 Kings 5:1–16; 9:10–28.

9. Joshua 9:3–27; 2 Samuel 21:1–14.

10. Genesis 39–41.

11. Numbers 20:14–21.

12. 2 Kings 12:17–21. An evil king of Israel, Menahem, also paid off Pul, king of Assyria. 2 Kings 15:17–19.

13. Exodus 22:18–21; 23:20–23; 32; Leviticus 24:10–24; Deuteronomy 4:15ff.; 6:13; 13; 16:21; 21:21; 22:21–24; Judges 8:33–35; 10:6–12:7; 1 Samuel 7:2–17; 12:1–25; 1 Kings 16:1–18; 2 Kings 22–23; 2 Chronicles 25:14–15; Daniel 1:1–21.

14. Joshua 6; 1 Samuel 15; 2 Samuel 8, 10.

15. John 2:12–23.

16. 1 John 4.

17. Galatians 5:16–26. See also Matthew 7:15–20.

18. Luke 24:45–49.

Chapter 8: Proclaiming the Truth

1. Allan Bloom, *The Closing of the American Mind* (New York: Simon and Schuster, 1987). Bloom's book discusses the intellectually inhibiting dangers of relativism. Another is Alasdair McIntyre, *After Virtue* (South Bend, Ind.: Notre Dame Press, 1986).

2. William Wilberforce, *Real Christianity* (Portland, Oreg.: Multnomah Press, 1982), 69.

3. John 14:6. See also 1 Samuel 4:1–7:1; Nehemiah 13; Esther; Psalm 9, 115, 135; Jeremiah 1:11–19; 19:1–5; Daniel 3, 6; Jonah 3, 4; Nahum; Matthew 6:7–8; John 15:1–17.

4. Luke 2:41–50; 7:37–50; John 4:1–42; 1 Corinthians 10:23–33. There is also a sense, especially in some Old Testament passages, that God used the conflict with other world views as a way of testing the people of God. See Judges 2:6–3:5; 1 Kings 17:7–24.

5. John Hick is perhaps the foremost proponent of this position. See his article "Religious Pluralism" in *The Encyclopedia of Relig-*

ion. See also Paul Knittner, *No Other Name* (Maryknoll, N.Y.: Orbis Press, 1986).

6. Catholic theologian Karl Rahner is a good example of this position. He suggested the concept of the "anonymous Christian" to describe those in other religions who achieve Christian salvation without knowing it.

7. Almost all of the major figures in church history were exclusivists—Augustine, Aquinas, Luther, Calvin, Wesley, Edwards, and Barth; the majority of modern theologians hold this position as well.

8. See Robert Short, *The Gospel from Outer Space* (San Francisco: Harper & Row, 1983), for a good discussion of the religious implications of the "Star Wars" trilogy.

9. William Whalen, "Reincarnation: Why Some People Expect to Make a Comeback," *U.S. Catholic* (Aug. 1988), 33–39.

10. *Chicago Tribune* (May 25, 1989), 21; *Time* magazine (May 8, 1989), 89.

11. For a good article and description of the New Age, see Kenneth Paul Kramer, "The Newest New Age," *The Catholic World* (May/June 1989), 100–5. It is interesting also to note that most college youth in the United States hold unfavorable views of the New Age. According to a Gallup poll, "Among U.S. college students who have heard or read about the New Age movement, unfavorable views of the movement outweigh favorable opinion by a more than 3-to-1 margin." See *Emerging Trends* (Dec. 1988), 1.

Chapter 9: Principles of Proclaiming the Truth

1. Richard Baxter, *The Reformed Pastor* (Portland, Oreg.: Multnomah Press, 1983).

2. Luke 12:49–53.

3. See John 15:18–16:4.

4. There are limits, of course, with whom you can have a conversation. One is reminded of the old Turkish fable of the fox and the wolf. The fox deceived the wolf, telling him that if he delivered a letter to the heads of the village, they would give him food to bring back. When the wolf reached the village, the dogs fell upon him, biting and wounding him. When he returned in a sad plight, the fox

said to him: "Why did you not show your letter?" "I did show it," was the reply, "but there were a thousand dogs who did not know the handwriting."

5. T. S. Eliot, *Murder in the Cathedral*, part 1.

6. 1 Corinthians 3:6.

7. Lesslie Newbigin, *Mission in Christ's Way* (Geneva, Switzerland: WCC, 1987), 19–20.

8. 1 Samuel 13:1–14:52; 15:1–35; 28:1–25; 31:1–13. See also the story of Ahab, 1 Kings 20:1–43.

9. Acts 19:23; 20:38.

10. Richard Mouw, "Christian Theology and Cultural Plurality," *The Scottish Bulletin of Evangelical Theology* (Autumn 1987), 195.

11. *Real Christianity* (Portland, Oreg.: Multnomah Press, 1982), 69.

12. Konstantin Stanislavski, *An Actor Prepares* (New York: Theatre Arts Books, 1984), 31–33.

Chapter 10: Evangelical Pluralism

1. Judges 2:22.

SELECT BIBLIOGRAPHY

Abe, Masao. *Zen and Western Thought*. Cambridge: Harvard University Press, 1985.

Ahlstrom, Sydney. *A Religious History of the American People*. New Haven: Yale University Press, 1972.

Alexander, Brooks. *Spirit Channeling: Evaluating the Latest in New Age Spiritism*. Downers Grove, Ill.: InterVarsity Press, 1988.

Aquinas, Thomas. *Summa Theologica*. New York: Random House, 1945.

Baird, Robert. *Category Formation and the History of Religions*. The Hague, Netherlands: Mouton, 1971.

Barrett, David, ed. *The World Christian Encyclopedia*. New York: Oxford University Press, 1982.

Barth, Karl. *Church Dogmatics*. Edinburgh: T. & T. Clark, 1975.

Bellah, Robert. *Habits of the Heart*. San Francisco: Harper & Row, 1985.

Calvin, John. *Institutes of the Christian Religion*. Philadelphia: Westminster Press, 1960.

Colson, Charles. *Kingdoms in Conflict*. Grand Rapids: Zondervan Publishing House, 1987.

Cousins, Norman. *In God We Trust*. New York: Harper & Brothers, 1958.

Cragg, Kenneth. *The Call of the Minaret*. Maryknoll, N.Y.: Orbis Books, 1985.

Cragg, Kenneth, and Marston Speight. *The House of Islam*. Berkeley, Calif.: Wadsworth, 1988.

Dasgupta, Surendra Nath. *A History of Indian Philosophy*. Cambridge, England: Cambridge University Press, 1922–55.

Dumoulin, Heinrich, and John Moraldo. *The Cultural, Political, and Religious Significance of Buddhism in the Modern World*. New York: Macmillan, 1976.

Embree, Ainslie. *The Hindu Tradition*. New York: Random House, 1972.

Embree, Ainslie, and Stephen Hay. *Sources of Indian Tradition*. New York: Columbia University Press, 1988.

Fields, Rick. *How the Swans Came to the Lake: A Narrative History of Buddhism in America*. Boulder, Colo.: Shambhala, 1981.

Gaustad, Edwin Scott. *A Documentary History of Religion in America Since 1865*. Grand Rapids: Eerdmans, 1983.

———. *A Religious History of America*. New York: Harper & Row, 1966.

Haddad, Yvonne, and Adair Lummis. *Islamic Values in the United States*. New York: Oxford University Press, 1987.

Henry, Carl F. H. *God, Revelation and Authority*. Waco, Tex.: Word Books, 1982.

———. *Twilight of a Great Civilization: The Drift Toward Neo-Paganism*. Westchester, Ill.: Crossway Books, 1988.

Herberg, Will. *Protestant, Catholic, and Jew*. Chicago: University of Chicago Press, 1983.

Hopkins, Thomas. *The Hindu Religious Tradition*. Berkeley, Calif.: Wadsworth, 1971.

Hudson, Winthrop. *Religion in America.* New York: Macmillan, 1987.

Hunter, James Davison. *Evangelicalism: The Coming Generation.* Chicago: University of Chicago Press, 1987.

Huszar, George, Henry Littlefield, and Arthur Littlefield. *Basic American Documents.* Ames, Iowa: Littlefield, Adams, 1953.

Layman, Emma McCloy. *Buddhism in America.* Chicago: Nelson Hall, 1976.

Lippy, Charles, and Peter Williams. *Encyclopedia of the American Religious Experience.* New York: Charles Scribner's Sons, 1988.

Marsden, George. *Fundamentalism in American Culture: The Shaping of Twentieth Century Evangelicalism.* New York: Oxford University Press, 1980.

Marty, Martin. *Pilgrims in Their Own Land: 500 Years of Religion in America.* Boston: Little, Brown, 1984.

Mead, Sidney. *The Old Religion in the Brave New World: Reflections on the Relation Between Christendom and the Republic.* Berkeley, Calif.: University of California Press, 1977.

Melton, J. Gordon. *The Encyclopedia of American Religions.* Detroit: Gale Research, 1989.

Murray, John Courtney. *We Hold These Truths.* Kansas City: Sheed and Ward, 1985.

Nazir-Ali, Michael. *Islam: A Christian Perspective.* Westminster, Pa.: John Knox Press, 1984.

Neill, Stephen. *Christian Faith and Other Faiths.* Downers Grove, Ill.: InterVarsity Press, 1984.

Neuhaus, Richard John. *The Naked Public Square.* Grand Rapids: Eerdmans, 1984.

Newbigin, Lesslie. *Foolishness to the Greeks*. Grand Rapids: Eerdmans, 1986.

Niebuhr, H. Richard. *Christ and Culture*. San Francisco: Harper & Row, 1951.

————. *The Nature and Destiny of Man*. New York: Charles Scribner's Sons, 1964.

Noll, Mark, ed. *Eerdmans' Handbook to Christianity in America*. Grand Rapids: Eerdmans, 1983.

Noll, Mark. *One Nation Under God*. San Francisco: Harper & Row, 1988.

O'Flaherty, Wendy. *Hindu Myths*. New York: Penguin Books, 1975.

Pfeffer, Leo. *Church, State, and Freedom*. Dobbs Ferry, N.Y.: Oceana Press, 1988.

————. *Creeds in Competition: A Creative Force in American Culture*. Westport, Conn.: Greenwood Press, 1978.

Plato. *The Republic*. New York: Tudor, 1928.

Prebish, Charles. *American Buddhism*. Belmont, Calif.: Duxbury Press, 1979.

Radhakrishnan, S. *Indian Religions*. Columbia, Mo.: South Asia Books, 1979.

Rahman, Fazlur. *Islam*. Chicago: University of Chicago Press, 1979.

Rahula, Walpola. *What the Buddha Taught*. New York: Grove Press, 1976.

Reichley, James. *Religion in American Public Life*. Washington, D.C.: The Brookings Institution, 1985.

Roof, Wade Clark, and William McKinney. *American Mainline Religion: Its Changing Shape and Future*. New Brunswick, N.J.: Rutgers University Press, 1987.

Smith, Wilfred Cantwell. *The Meaning and End of Religion*. New York: Harper & Row, 1978.

Stokes, Anson Phelps. *Church and State in the United States*. New York: Harper & Brothers, 1950.

Stott, John R. *Between Two Worlds*. Grand Rapids: Eerdmans, 1982.

Streng, Frederick. *Understanding Religious Life*. Berkeley, Calif.: Wadsworth, 1985.

Swidler, Leonard, ed. *Religious Liberty and Human Rights in Nations and in Religions*. Philadelphia: Ecumenical Press, 1986.

Tocqueville, Alexis de. *Democracy in America*. New York: Harper & Row, 1966.

Wells, David F. *God the Evangelist: How the Holy Spirit Works to Bring Men and Women to Faith*. Grand Rapids: Eerdmans, 1987.

Woodberry, J. Dudley. *Muslims and Christians on the Emmaus Road*. Monrovia, Calif.: MARC, 1989.

Zaehner, R. C., ed. *Hindu Scriptures*. New York: Oxford University Press, 1978.

Zaehner, R. C. *Hinduism*. New York: Oxford University Press, 1962.